THIS
DRINKING
NATION

FOUR WINDS PRESS ⋛⋚ *New York*

MAXWELL MACMILLAN CANADA   *Toronto*

MAXWELL MACMILLAN INTERNATIONAL   *New York Oxford Singapore Sydney*

"The Worship of
Bacchus, or
The Drinking Customs
of Society," as depicted
by George Cruikshank
in 1864
(Library of Congress)

THIS

DRINKING

NATION

JONATHAN HARRIS

ALSO BY JONATHAN HARRIS

Drugged Athletes
Drugged America

*Special thanks to James Kirby Martin, Professor of History
at the University of Houston, for checking the facts in this
book and sharing his insightful reading of the material*

Four Winds Press
Macmillan Publishing Company
866 Third Avenue
New York, NY 10022
Maxwell Macmillan Canada, Inc.
1200 Eglinton Avenue East
Suite 200
Don Mills, Ontario M3C 3N1
Macmillan Publishing Company is part of the
Maxwell Communication Group of Companies.
First edition
Printed and bound in the United States of America
10 9 8 7 6 5 4 3 2 1
The text of this book is set in Galliard.
Book design by Andrea Schneeman

Harris, Jonathan, date.
  This drinking nation / Jonathan Harris.—1st ed.
     p.   cm.
  Includes bibliographical references (p.   ) and index.
  ISBN 0-02-742744-7
  1. Drinking of alcoholic beverages—United States—History—
     Juvenile literature.   2. Alcoholism—United States—History—
     Juvenile literature.   [1. Alcohol.   2. Alcoholism.]   I. Title.
  HV5066.H36   1994
  394.1'3'0973—dc20   94-9776

To my first grandchild:
The choice is yours.
Choose freely among
the blessings of this nation.
                    —J.H.

CONTENTS

THIS
DRINKING
NATION

1   SKETCHES OF THIS DRINKING NATION

1

America has always been a battleground. On one side have stood the "wets," who enjoy drinking alcoholic beverages and oppose all efforts by government or any other agency to put limits on their freedom to drink. On the other side have been the "drys," some of whom seek to promote moderation in drinking, while others seek to prohibit it altogether.

The following "sketches" from our history tell the stories of some of the interesting characters who have carried on this battle from its beginning to recent times.

1660s Joseph Birch was well-known as the town drunk in colonial Dorchester, Massachusetts. In 1669 the Puritan authorities twice ordered him to find some kind of employment. The official order directed him "to put himself in an orderly way of living . . . or else to expect that he will be presented to the Court for disorderly living." The warning had little effect, for as the years passed Birch was arrested again and again for drunkenness and for ignoring the order to find work.

Despite the reputation of the Puritans for strictness, the record indicates that Birch suffered formal punishment only once. On that occasion he got off with a fine and a few hours of sitting in the stocks (a wooden framework before which the prisoner sat while his legs and feet were held fast; it was in a public place and the prisoner was subject to all kinds of public scorn).

Most of the times he was arrested, Birch solemnly and publicly promised to mend his ways. The authorities tried to help him. One time, for example, when he was arrested after a drunken binge he made his usual pledge to sober up, whereupon a job was found for him and "he was granted liberty to cut wood." The record does not tell us whether this particular citizen of the Puritan commonwealth of Massachusetts ever did quit drinking for very long.

1864 In the summer of 1864 President Abraham Lincoln was anxiously searching for a general with the experience and the fighting spirit that were needed for command of the Army of the Potomac. This Union army encompassed all the forces then fighting General Robert E. Lee's Army of Northern Virginia in the eastern theater of the Civil War. Every general Lincoln had entrusted with the Army of the Potomac since the war began in 1861 had either been defeated by Lee or had been disappointingly cautious about attacking him.

Lincoln finally selected General Ulysses S. Grant, who had recently won a series of notable victories over the Confederates in the west.

The ink was scarcely dry on Lincoln's order appointing Grant when the whispers started. "Grant," the president was warned repeatedly, "is a confirmed drunkard. He's even said to have been drunk during some important battles." "I only wish I knew what brand of whiskey he drinks," Lincoln replied to his informants. "I'd send a barrel or so to some of my other generals!"

1879–1898 Frances Willard came to national prominence as the first dean of women at Northwestern University. In 1879 she was elected president of the Woman's Christian Temperance Union. The WCTU, along with other reform-minded organizations, was waging battle to rid America of poverty, crime, corruption, mistreatment of prisoners and the insane, and a variety of other evils.

But for Willard and the WCTU, drinking and drunkenness were the worst sources of evil. The saloon was the hateful den of sin that led men to drink and debauchery, and the WCTU was determined to do away with it.

Willard was convinced that drinking was dangerous to women's rights, their security and morality. She called the WCTU's antisaloon campaign the "politics of the mother heart." Under her leadership the WCTU was the foremost organization among several that fought successfully to get Prohibition laws passed in several states.

Willard organized the WCTU into forty smooth-running departments, each with its own reform specialty. She died in 1898, by which time she had begun to doubt the social value of Prohibition. She also recognized that alcohol abuse resulted from broader social problems. By that time the WCTU had hundreds of thousands of members.

1899–1911 One of the most colorful figures ever to do battle against drinking was a burly, pugnacious woman named Carry Nation. Where other women were content to advance the cause by suddenly appearing in groups at the entrances to saloons and taverns, waving antiliquor banners, praying, and singing hymns, Carry Nation felt it necessary to go much further.

One day in 1899 she dared to invade the actual interior of a saloon—where no respectable lady was customarily seen. Without further ado she started to smash up the bar and other saloon furnishings, using a small hatchet, which she had brought with her for this purpose.

This was the start of a nationwide campaign of what became known as "hatchetation." As she extended her destructive escapades ever further, she garnered reams of publicity. Carry Nation reveled in her newfound fame, and took profitable advantage of it by selling souvenir hatchets.

At first her campaign won the support of Protestant leaders and the largest of the national antiliquor bodies, the Woman's Christian Temperance Union. Nation herself became a successful traveling lecturer.

But eventually she became a kind of joke. Church leaders and WCTU officials began to look upon her as an embarrassment. Distillers wrote her humorous letters, thanking her for giving their liquors such splendid free advertising. Soon saloons were featuring "Carry Nation cocktails."

Carry Nation died in a mental hospital in 1911.

1883–1935 Billy Sunday was an ex-baseball player who became one of America's most popular evangelists. He was an uncompromising foe of drinking and saloons. One of his many biographers called him the "greatest of God's warriors."

From 1883 to 1888 he played center field for the Chicago White Stockings, as the team was then called. Over the next three years, he played for Pittsburgh and Philadelphia. Then he quit the diamond and in a few years launched his unparalleled career as a preacher of the gospel.

Starting in rural areas and in small-town churches and tents, he eventually was holding whole series of meetings in all the larger towns and cities. Tabernacles were built for him that accommodated many thousands of people. He employed professional musicians, huge choirs, and every other conceivable means of enhancing the emotional power of his sermons.

Collections were taken only at the last meeting in each locale, but his audiences were almost always generous. Sunday is thought to have amassed a sizable personal fortune.

He preached in a wildly uninhibited style. At unpredictable moments he would perform all sorts of startling acrobatics, pound the rostrum or his palm, pace back and forth, scream, yell, weep, laugh, even pretend to be boxing with the devil.

His theology was a primitive kind of nineteenth-century fundamentalism, already out-of-date. He denounced not only drinking and spending time in saloons but all other time-wasting pleasures—though he never mentioned baseball.

Among his most unforgettable sermons was one called "The Famous Booze Sermon." He repeated this in one variant or another to hundreds of audiences, always to wild acclaim. Speaking of the liquor traffic, he called it "the most damnable, corrupt institution that ever wriggled out of Hell and fastened itself on the public." To him, fighting the accursed beast of alcohol was as elemental and simple as good and right versus evil, poverty, and crime.

His style is well illustrated by the following excerpt from his denunciation of the saloon:

> The saloon is an infidel. It has no faith in God, has no religion. . . . It cocks the high-wayman's pistol. It puts the rope into the hands of the mob. It is the anarchist of the world, and its red flag is dyed with the blood of women and children. It sent the bullet through the body of Lincoln. It nerved the arm that sent the bullets through Garfield and William McKinley. Yes, it is a murderer. I tell you that the curse of God Almighty is on the saloon.

Abolish the liquor traffic, Sunday stormed, and you would cut down on mental illness, crime, troubled families. He recited pitiful story after story of how liquor had ruined individuals' lives (many of these heart-wrenching stories were undoubtedly made up on the spot, but his listeners oohed and aahed and wept anyway).

Sunday's sermons also included a detailed and truly sickening description of liquor's effects on the body. Since he actually knew little about the subject, much of this, too, was made up, but nonetheless horrifying.

He mounted toward his climax with an appeal to support proven antiliquor politicians, to fight the saloons so that they could not tempt husbands and sons and "send them home maudlin, brutish, devilish, vomiting, stinking, bear-eyed, bloated-faced drunkards."

Billy Sunday's greatest triumph came in December 1917: passage by Congress, and ratification by the states in the record time of thirteen months, of the Eighteenth

Amendment to the U.S. Constitution. Backed by suitable legislation in 1920, it outlawed liquor throughout the country. Billy Sunday's thousands of adoring fans forever after credited him, quite properly, with a key role in this victory of Prohibition. Billy Sunday lived, however, to see Prohibition repealed in 1933.

1920–1933 Both men were short and fat. They often wore outlandish or comical disguises when going into action. They looked like anything but what they were: two of the toughest, most widely publicized, hardest-working, most spectacularly effective, most absolutely honest agents employed by the U.S. government to enforce the Eighteenth, or Prohibition, Amendment.

Their names were Izzy Einstein and Moe Smith. Stories about their daring exploits appeared in the newspapers so often that after a while their names were paired off simply as "Izzy and Moe."

Together they confiscated millions of dollars' worth of illegal liquor. They carried out thousands of raids on stills (whiskey-making equipment) and speakeasies (illegal bars and saloons). They arrested more than four thousand bootleggers (makers and/or sellers of illegal liquor).

The trouble was that they were in the headlines so frequently that their superiors in the federal government's Prohibition Bureau began to feel that it was downright undignified. And so in the late 1920s Izzy and Moe were fired.

All their efforts, as well as those of thousands of other Prohibition agents, proved futile in the end. Prohibition was repealed in 1933. The "Noble Experiment" lasted just thirteen years. Americans could relax and once again enjoy a legal drink.

1 9 2 □ s – 1 9 4 7 In the wide-open Chicago of the Roaring Twenties, Prohibition had relatively little effect. There was plenty of bootleg liquor. Johnny Torrio ran the city's biggest bootleg operation and a lot of the town's other rackets.

But by the mid-1920s Torrio, having been badly wounded in one of Chicago's unceasing gangland wars, was anxious to retire.

He carefully picked Al Capone to take over. Capone was a Brooklyn gangster renowned for his murderous ruthlessness. He had moved to Chicago to join Torrio's gang shortly before 1920. He had risen rapidly through the ranks to become Torrio's right-hand man.

Now unchallenged boss of the Torrio mob, Capone declared war on the remaining rival gangs in Chicago. In a series of bloody killings and massacres, he very nearly wiped them out.

His most infamous act was the St. Valentine's Day Massacre in 1929. He had a few of his men masquerade as uniformed and plainclothes policemen. They invaded a garage belonging to the North Side gang, behaved as if they were making routine arrests, lined up seven men facing a wall, and raked them all with submachine gunfire.

Capone considerably expanded Torrio's former empire of crime. At the Capone mob's peak of power, its varied rackets, including bootlegging, prostitution, and gambling, brought in several hundreds of millions of dollars a year.

Meanwhile, by bribing corrupt police, judges, and other officials at all levels of the city government, Capone fended off all interference by local authorities.

He had no such influence with the federal government, however. Painstaking analysis by Prohibition Bureau and

Treasury Department accountants of his income, coupled with his arrogant refusal to file income tax forms over many years, led to his downfall. In October 1931 he was convicted of income tax evasion and Prohibition law violations, and was sentenced to eleven years in prison. He spent most of his sentence in Alcatraz, then America's toughest maximum-security prison.

Capone got time off for good behavior and was released in 1939 a sick and broken man. He died in 1947 of general paralysis of the insane, caused by a syphilitic infection he had gotten long before.

1920s–1935 Bill W. (everyone in this sketch shall remain anonymous, for reasons that will be clear later) was a highly successful Wall Street stock analyst in the 1920s. In that age of rip-roaring stock market speculation, with the prices of stocks seemingly on an endless upward curve, most of Bill's investments seemed almost magically to turn into golden profits.

He rapidly built up an impressive "paper" fortune. Paper, that is, because it consisted largely of stocks and other securities. As long as their value remained high, he was a rich man. Bill had already become a big drinker. In those rosy years of prosperity, he had reached the point where he drank all day and kept it up most nights. He quarreled with any friends who questioned his drinking. He was a lone wolf now. There were frequent scenes with his wife as well, but she remained loyal.

Then came Black Tuesday, in October 1929, when stock values suddenly plunged to catastrophic lows. Thousands of investors lost every penny. Bill, too, was wiped out financially.

One morning in 1935 as he sat drinking alone, he got an unexpected phone call. It was an old school friend, who sounded cheerful and completely *sober*. Bill hadn't seen him in that condition in years. He invited the friend to come over at once. Bill's plan was to get drunk with his old pal and have a good time, as they used to.

His visitor arrived, looking healthy and fit. He bewildered Bill by refusing a drink. He was, somehow, different. He explained: He had "gotten religion." Two months earlier he had been told of a simple religious idea and a practical program of action. He hadn't had a drink since. The program *worked*!

The visitor had come to share the experience with Bill. And Bill, having reached the depths of despair, was willing to listen.

Though Bill rejected the conventional concept of a personal God, he did believe in a Higher Power, a Supreme Intelligence that had shaped this world and ruled over it. His friend said he had put himself in God's hands. God had saved him from drunkenness and ruin when he could do nothing for himself. Bill could choose his own concept of God or Higher Power.

For the first time in his life, Bill admitted that he was powerless against the lure of alcohol. He made up his mind to turn himself completely over to God's power.

And he stopped drinking, then and there.

Together Bill and his friend decided that they had a responsibility to spread their message among other alcoholics, and to help them in every way they could. They determined to establish a fellowship open to all who were struggling against the hellish temptations of alcohol.

They named the fellowship Alcoholics Anonymous.

2 ⋮ DRINKING AMERICA: YESTERDAY AND TODAY

(previous page)
A "beer garden" in
Interlochen, Michigan,
1942
(Library of Congress)

2

THE ROLE OF DRINKING IN HISTORY

Revealing insights into a nation's social history can be gained by tracing its drinking patterns. The ideas that people had about drinking gradually evolved in various ways as the nation matured. The changes in these notions shed light on how Americans thought, lived, and spent their leisure. Why the people indulged in heavy drinking at certain periods and less drinking at others, and why they experimented with a total ban on drinking at still another stage, reflects their economic, social, cultural, and intellectual history.

This book tells the story of drinking in America. It attempts to flesh out that story by placing it within the context of the broader historical development of the nation. It focuses on the long struggle between the "wets," who favored drinking, and the "drys," who either opposed drinking altogether or sought some way to keep it within moderate limits.

America's drinking history started out differently from other nations'. The colonists who first settled this land arrived with their drinking preferences already formed in the old country. They knew what they were used to drinking, and at what times of the day, and on what holidays.

Living conditions in the New World, the nature of the soil, and numerous other factors made it necessary to adjust to changed circumstances. The colonists soon developed American tastes, and favored certain beverages developed in America, along with the old European favorites.

A particularly noteworthy feature of the story of drinking in the United States is the short-lived victory of the drys. Through long and mighty effort and careful organizing, they succeeded in imposing national Prohibition in 1919. They were convinced that their achievement marked the beginning of a great and lasting purification of America. But, for a variety of reasons, Prohibition lasted only thirteen years.

The Prohibition period (1920–1933), though brief, was one of the most colorful in our history, and we shall take an especially close look at it. Prohibition transformed the nation in many ways. One of its more sinister legacies was the Mafia. That organized crime society is still among the most powerful forces in the criminal world today.

Alcohol consumption increased in the 1950s and early 1970s more sharply than at any other time in our history. Then, starting about 1980, drinking by most groups within the population went on the decline. The reasons are varied and complex. Not all experts cite the same causes. Chapter 9 offers a detailed analysis of the various explanations that have been proposed.

There is agreement on one worrisome subject, however. That is the persistence of young people in ignoring the national trend toward cutting down on consumption of alcoholic beverages. In general, with few exceptions, the young have kept up their relatively high drinking rate.

Expert opinion is divided on the reasons for this, too.

This is all the more remarkable in light of the tendency among one element of youth to moderate some of its drinking habits. College students nowadays seem to be abandoning many of their former ways. Campuses are no longer scenes of uninhibited drinking contests. Spring break in particular has become a far more moderate time of relaxation than it had been.

Still, despite all the welcome news about declines in various groups' drinking rates, there is little cause for complacency. A few typical examples taken from recent surveys should suffice to show that drinking remains a serious problem.

Mothers Against Drunk Driving, or MADD, for example, recently ran a study that produced the startling finding that no fewer than two of every five Americans know someone either killed or injured by a drunk driver. An even higher percentage—55 percent—know someone convicted of drunk driving.

Another group surveyed by MADD was asked to rate what they considered safety problems. Almost every person who was asked that question cited the influence of alcohol on drivers.

Over 70 percent of those polled approved the use of sobriety checkpoints (where police check every driver passing through a certain point on a highway for drunkenness) to screen out impaired drivers. Nearly six out of nineteen persons questioned came out in favor of tougher penalties for repeat offenders.

It is true that during the 1980s the percentage of drivers killed in drinking-related auto accidents dropped sharply. This decline was steepest among sixteen- to twenty-year-olds. It reflected the raising of the minimum legal drinking age to twenty-one by many states. Since 1987 that number has stubbornly stalled at 40 percent.

More recently, the proportion of alcohol-related fatal accidents among young drivers has started to rise again. This fact should sound a loud alarm bell, for the number is climbing dangerously close to previous record levels.

Law enforcement officials have a broad range of means available for deterring drunk driving. The simplest and most effective is to take the drunk driver's car keys, but for various legal reasons this is not always feasible in some states.

The police use a variety of techniques. Most common is the passive alcohol sensor, or Breathalyzer. It is a small screening device that analyzes the content of air near the mouth. Police use it to detect alcohol-impaired drivers.

Some police departments run seminars for bar and restaurant workers, teaching them about alcohol's effects and training them to detect signs of impairment. The law in many states prohibits bars and restaurants from serving alcoholic beverages to intoxicated patrons.

More practical, and much more widely adopted among today's drivers, is the "designated driver" concept. Before the start of a festive evening, one of the group is chosen who pledges not to drink. Afterward, he or she drives everyone home.

MANY WAYS OF THINKING ABOUT DRINKING

The American people have never united around any single opinion about drinking. While about one-third of the population are teetotalers, the majority accepts a wide variety of drinking patterns. Some tolerate the notion of "getting loaded" at certain kinds of parties (e.g., college fraternity parties, Christmas parties, New Year's Eve parties, et cetera). Others see heavy drinking by a man as proof that he is "macho" or a "real man."

Americans are quite accustomed to spending large amounts every year on alcoholic beverages. At the same time, they have accepted the concept of alcoholism as a disease. This acceptance has not prevented them from looking down upon alcoholics and treating them as outcasts.

The statistical evidence is not complete enough to allow detailed comparisons between the 1990s and previous decades. It does support the conclusion that the amount of drinking in the U.S. has been declining slowly since the 1980s.

DECLINE IN DRINKING

In 1987, *Time* magazine conducted a poll with noteworthy results. It measured drinking by persons at least eighteen years old. The poll found that no more than 67 percent drank any alcoholic beverages. One-third of those who admitted they drank said they had cut down on their drinking. Just 6 percent had increased it.

These poll results are borne out by figures compiled by the distilling industry. The industry reported that annual liquor consumption per capita had declined 15 percent between 1974 and 1985. The same source indicated that consumption of hard liquor dropped 8 percent in the one-year period from 1990 to 1991. Drinkers were switching to less potent wines and beer.

Wine purchases rose during the 1960s and 1970s, but dropped sharply by the mid-1980s. From 1990 to 1991 the

Wine Institute reported a drop of nearly 10 percent. Major vintners were resorting to new products, such as wine coolers (a mix of light wine and fruit juice), to boost their sales.

Beer drinking, too, was down, about 2 percent. Only low-alcohol and alcohol-free wines and beers, sparkling ciders, and seltzer waters were reporting rising sales.

Among the reasons given for the general decline were the economic recession of the late 1980s and early 1990s, a new federal excise tax on alcoholic beverages, the widespread development of a new health and fitness consciousness, and a growing awareness of the health hazards of excessive drinking.

How did Americans arrive at this contradictory and confused state of affairs? How did our drinking patterns develop during the long stretch since the colonial days? What changes have the American people gone through in their attitudes toward drinking? For answers to these questions we must now take a look at America's past.

3 : BORN DRINKING
(1607–1836)

(previous page)
Soldiers and Indians revel
at a French fort. Although
the English soldiers here
are looking on the French
with disapproval, they, too,
had their own drinking
habits brought over to the
New World from Europe.
(Library of Congress)

3

. . . .

European Habits

The early colonists brought their European drinking habits with them to the New World. They settled in Virginia, Massachusetts, and New Amsterdam (now New York City). First they had to assure themselves of adequate food supplies, shelter, and protection from the Indians. Then they planned to produce some sort of alcoholic beverage.

The very first group of colonists, who landed at Jamestown, Virginia, in 1607, included a number of beer drinkers. They soon found that their skills were not equal to the task of brewing an acceptable beer. Scarcely three years after arriving on these shores, they had to advertise in London for two brewers.

As for the Pilgrims aboard the *Mayflower,* they took care to lay in a supply of beer to sustain them during the long voyage. By the time they landed, they had drunk up their entire supply.

The ship's crew still had a supply of beer for the return voyage, but refused to share it. Had they been more generous, they would undoubtedly have run out of beer and have had to drink water. This they were unwilling to do, as the water supply on long voyages frequently turned foul-tasting and was correctly regarded as a possible source of disease.

Eventually the *Mayflower*'s captain relented and gave the Pilgrims some beer from the crew's stock, but it was certainly not enough for the entire winter. The settlers were inevitably driven to drink the local water—which they were astonished to find excellent.

The first crop the Pilgrims hoped to grow in the new settlement was barley. Some of this would have been used for food; the rest served for brewing. When they found that barley did not thrive in the rocky New England soil, they planted apple trees. Juice from the apples could be fermented into an alcoholic form of cider known as applejack.

The brewing of beer began to develop throughout the Massachusetts Bay Colony. Home brew concocted by housewives provided part of the settlers' needs. After a time, commercial brewers provided more. Some tavern owners brewed their own beer as well. Imported beer was available, but was much more expensive than the domestic varieties.

Somewhat later, in 1640, the governor of the Dutch colony at New Amsterdam, Willem Kieft, set up the first distillery in America, on Staten Island. He then, very logically, established the first tavern.

It was not long before every town and village could boast of its own hospitable taverns or public houses and its welcoming inns for travelers.

The British won control of New Amsterdam from the Dutch in 1664. By that time, tastes were changing. Imported rum was replacing beer as the colonists' favorite beverage. The British promptly converted Kieft's distillery from its original brandywine and gin production to rum.

Rum had a strength of 100 to 200 proof (50 to 100 percent alcohol), which made it a powerful beverage indeed.

FROM "GIFT OF GOD" TO "DEMON RUM"

Thus, the evidence is clear that America was a drinking nation from its very birth. Alcoholic beverages were regarded at that time as healthful and nutritious substances given by God and vital to the proper functioning of man. Bottles of whiskey were often incorporated into the cornerstones of new churches as tokens of thanksgiving for God's love. Leading authorities urged moderate use, however, and drunkenness was universally condemned.

The colonists' custom was to pause for drinks several times a day. The morning started with a "dram," and the day continued with drinks taken periodically. Beer and/or cider were usually found on the family dinner table. Drinks were even served to children, though probably in smaller, diluted quantities.

In some parts of the country, notably in the South, drinking was an accepted part of the political process. Candidates for elective office were expected to "treat" the voters with free drinks. There were even drinks to be had at some polling places, to reward the voter who might have traveled dusty roads for many weary miles to get there.

But from Massachusetts to Virginia, drinking for some good citizens gradually began to change from a harmless indulgence to an addictive habit. What had for so long been innocently thought of as a gift from Heaven was showing its other face as "Demon Rum." Among the respected groups that condemned liquor in all its forms were the Quakers and the Methodists.

As early as 1639 an effort was made to combat drunkenness in Massachusetts by prohibiting the drinking of "healths" to anyone, and the offering of toasts on any occasion. The "useless custom" of repeated drinking of healths was known to be the cause of much excessive drinking.

Another method used by the authorities to fight drunkenness was to forbid the selling of more than one half-pint of wine to any person at one time. This rule soon proved ineffective, as alcoholic beverages of all kinds were sold—and continued to be sold—in many taverns, in tankards larger than mere half-pints, and also in larger quantities.

THE TRIANGLE TRADE

Once the colonists were able to produce enough liquor for their domestic needs, they made alcoholic beverages an important commodity in their trade with other countries. Often short of cash, they carried on their trade by barter. No exchange of money took place.

The Pilgrims developed an active trade with Jamaica, exchanging such products as fish and timber for inexpensive Jamaican molasses. Fermenting molasses into rum was not difficult, and soon they were producing more than enough for their own use.

The Puritans gradually developed the notorious Triangle Trade: They shipped rum to Africa, where it was traded for slaves, who were in turn exchanged in the West Indies for molasses, which was made into rum in New England. Then the whole highly profitable process began again.

Within a few years the New England colonies were exporting 600,000 gallons of rum a year. Boston, Massachusetts, and Newport, Rhode Island, boasted thirty commercial distilleries each, and other New England towns were not far behind.

THE SPREAD OF DRUNKENNESS

With such a powerful and popular beverage as rum available cheaply and in abundance, it is not surprising that drinking and drunkenness began to spread rapidly among all classes and even all ages. Drinking was common on special occasions such as funerals, celebrations of new ministers' ordinations, and militia musters.

Most drinking, however, was done within the home, usually at mealtimes. On public occasions, on holidays, or generally when social drinking was called for, men gathered in the taverns. Women—respectable women, that is—were most definitely not welcome in these drinking places.

The authorities began to fear that uncontrolled drinking might lead to crime, wild behavior, and even civil disorder. Businessmen and farmers had long been accustomed to making drinks available to their workmen during the day. Now they became aware that drinking reduced labor's productivity.

By 1770, even as the Triangle Trade was mounting toward its peak, Americans were importing a million gallons of rum annually. They were themselves distilling another five million gallons. The colonists consumed no less than seven-eighths of this vast quantity.

As alcohol abuse and its harmful side effects spread, the notion that alcohol was probably poisonous in some way was gaining acceptance among the most advanced medical practitioners. Yet the virtues of alcohol continued to be widely believed in, and most physicians prescribed various alcoholic mixtures for toothache, broken limbs, colds, snakebite, and a whole variety of illnesses both physical and mental.

TAVERN REGULATION

With liquor becoming a major article of domestic trade and commerce, every aspect of the liquor trade was subjected to careful regulation by the colonial governments. Detailed legal codes specified what classes of citizens tavern keepers could sell to, at what hours and on what days, and even at what prices.

Drunkenness was a crime throughout the colonies. Liquor could not be sold to confirmed drunkards in Plymouth; Virginia law prohibited tavern keepers who might extend credit to drunkards from suing to collect the debt.

In 1681 Massachusetts's assembly of town deputies decided to strengthen the laws limiting drinking by tightening up the tavern licensing rules. They were determined to reduce the rapidly growing number of taverns throughout Massachusetts. They slashed the number from forty-five to twenty-four in Boston. All other towns could have only one tavern each, except six seaport towns. An unknown but sizable number of unlicensed establishments continued to operate, however. Eventually the deputies gave in to the popular will and issued more tavern licenses. Soon the number of taverns in Boston was back up to forty-three.

Taverns served many purposes. They were often the most convenient places for retail liquor purchases. Inns combined the functions of taverns and hotels. They were indispensable for travelers, often providing the towns' only food and lodging.

The problem was that while governing bodies might lay down all kinds of regulations, enforcement was weak. In 1695 the government of Massachusetts found it necessary to order all elected officials to enforce the laws with vigor. The order was accompanied by a warning to all officials against "taking any bribe, fee, received directly or indirectly" to conceal information about any applicant for a tavern license. Upon conviction for this or any similar crime, such officials would have to "pay three times the value . . . received as a bribe." Only pervasive corruption could have made such a dire warning necessary.

The ultimate futility of these various attempts to limit drinking is shown by the government's making only one more such effort. In 1712 the General Court of Massachusetts (the colony's legislature) passed a sweeping Act Against Intemperance. There was no further legislation on this subject during the entire eighteenth century, a tacit admission that popular resistance had proven stronger than the authorities' will to regulate.

Over the years many of the taverns evolved into active centers of political discussion. Both before and during the Revolution important ideas and principles concerning resistance to royal authority first took shape in taverns.

A TIME OF HEAVY DRINKING

By 1792 the United States supported an astonishing two thousand five hundred registered commercial distilleries.

Consumption of alcoholic beverages by an average American over fifteen years old that year is reliably estimated at about thirty-four gallons of beer and cider, slightly less than five gallons of distilled liquors, and less than one gallon of wine. These prodigious amounts add up to nearly six gallons of pure alcohol each year.

Behind the heavy drinking of the late eighteenth century lay the development of new American attitudes stemming from the Revolutionary era. Americans valued their recently won personal freedoms. They resented and rejected not only the old British governmental restraints but unreasonable restraints from any official source. They placed their faith in unfettered individualism. Among other freedoms, they insisted on the right to drink as they pleased.

Drinking almost became a patriotic act, especially when the liquor being drunk was American.

DEVELOPMENT OF THE
TEMPERANCE MOVEMENT

In a society where religion dominated daily living, it is not surprising that the Puritan church played a crucial role in dealing with cases of public drunkenness. Public drunkenness was regarded as a sin and therefore an offense against God.

Three methods of punishment were available: public warnings, suspension from church membership, and excommunication. The last was the most serious, for at least in theory it meant permanent banishment from all participation in church activities. Actually, the churches tended to be quite lenient. Drunks who promised to reform were usually forgiven, and those who had been deprived of church membership were readmitted after promising to stay sober.

Another example of negative attitudes toward drinking was the action taken in the 1730s by the governor of the colony of Georgia, James Oglethorpe. Acting with the approval of his English trustees, he banned use of "Rum, Brandies, Spirits, or Strong Waters" within the colony. The order proved extremely unpopular and gave rise to considerable smuggling from neighboring colonies. It was repealed after only seven years.

The first published work that attempted a serious scientific discussion of the dangers of drinking was written by a distinguished Philadelphia physician, Dr. Benjamin Rush. He was one of the patriots who had signed the Declaration of Independence in 1776.

Now, in 1784, he wrote the impressively titled *An Enquiry into the Effects of Spirituous Liquors upon the Human Mind and Body*. Rush expressly allowed for the use of such relatively mild potions as beer, wine, and cider. But he warned that hard liquors (rum, whiskey, and brandy) were the cause of many diseases.

The book was widely influential in its day. But Rush harbored no illusions about Americans' willingness to ignore the risks and go right on drinking as they pleased.

Though Rush's book was based on wide experience gained from his considerable medical practice, and marshaled the available evidence with great skill, it contained little strictly scientific evidence by modern standards.

One result of Rush's work was the formation a few years later of America's first temperance society. Organized at Saratoga, New York, in 1808, the Union Temperance Society's members pledged to abstain from all intoxicating beverages "excepting on the advice of a physician or in case of actual disease, also excepting wine at public dinners."

In 1826 several church groups and Bible and Tract societies joined together in the American Society for the

Promotion of Temperance (later the American Temperance Union). Other temperance societies sprang up all over the country. Many copied the Saratoga society's pledge of abstinence. By 1833 the union had about six thousand branches, with more than a million members.

Three years later the American Temperance Union adopted a more extreme position. It came out not only against the drinking of distilled liquor, but also against indulgence in wine, beer, cider, and all intoxicating beverages. The union insisted on total abstinence.

RELATIONS WITH NATIVE AMERICANS AND AFRICAN AMERICANS

Dealings with the Native Americans were a constant vexation for the colonists. Part of the problem was deciding how to control the Indians' access to liquor. The authorities were convinced that drunkenness among the Indians frequently led to violence against whites.

Actually, there was more to the story than that. In many cases the Native Americans had been deliberately plied with liquor by whites scheming to buy their land or hoping to trade for their furs, or by whites offering the Indians treaties that often were unfavorable to them.

A notable example was the Treaty of Easton, signed in 1758. Under its terms the Native Americans ceded vast areas of their territory in what is now Pennsylvania. They had been given copious quantities of liquor at every stage of the negotiations.

The Native Americans had never experienced alcohol before the coming of the Europeans. They had first been introduced to it when Henry Hudson gave gin to some

Indians of Manhattan Island in exchange for geographical information.

It was a relatively simple matter to get the Native Americans drunk and then to cheat them. All too often, violence was the ultimate result.

All of the colonies eventually enacted regulations controlling the sale of liquor to Indians. One common way of dealing with the problem was to license agents, who were usually given exclusive rights to sell liquor to the Native Americans under official supervision.

As the Indians became increasingly alert to the evil effects of alcohol, there were movements within some of the tribes to warn against drunkenness and even to promote abstinence. Native Americans on several occasions sought to get white officials to stop liquor from being brought into Indian territory. Some whites were sympathetic, but little was ever done to halt or even to reduce the liquor traffic.

One powerful reason is that the American fur companies got their entire profit from trading liquor for the Native Americans' pelts. There was no particular racial discrimination in this, as they dealt with the white fur trappers in exactly the same way.

For example: Around 1818 the American Fur Company traded with the Indians of Mackinaw. The Indians got whiskey that was a mixture of two gallons of spirits, thirty gallons of water, and unknown amounts of red pepper and tobacco. Exactly the same fraudulent mixture was traded to the white trappers. It cost three cents a gallon to make, and was sold for fifty cents a bottle. The company would have made far less profit without this kind of trading.

African Americans, too, were regarded as a potentially hostile element in the population. The fear of violence by them against whites was widespread and deep-rooted. In states with large African-American populations whites believed it crucially important always to be on guard against the possibility of slave insurrections. Liquor, if the slaves could get any without the masters' approval, might play a dangerous role.

Slaves were forbidden to obtain liquor from white men without the express permission of their masters, usually in written form. On certain holidays, most commonly after the crop had been harvested or during the Christmas season, slaves might be given one or even two days off from work, and they might be allotted a supply of liquor. This was regarded as a safe way to let the slaves vent any anger or grievances or other ill feelings they might have accumulated during the year. They were usually restricted to the slave quarters for such celebrations. Armed supervision by whites was, of course, close at hand.

No writings by African Americans of the colonial period expressing their feelings about drinking or drunkenness are known to exist. Their attitudes were probably best voiced later by the black abolitionist leader Frederick Douglass. He escaped from slavery during the early nineteenth century. Slave holidays, in Douglass's words, "represent the most effective means in the hands of the slaveholder in keeping down the spirit of insurrection."

Whites generally frowned upon drinking by free blacks as well. In the whites' imagination, drunken African Americans were regarded as prone to violence and capable of committing unspeakable acts.

Several slave insurrections actually did occur in the early 1800s, with many whites attacked and killed before the uprisings could be brought under control. There is no reli-

able evidence that these carefully organized and daringly exe-
cuted revolts owed any significant part of their inspiration to
liquor. Nevertheless, the belief was widely held among white
southerners that liquor was a causative factor in at least several of these revolts.

African Americans, enslaved or free, were not ordinarily
admitted to taverns or other establishments where liquor
was served to white men. A Connecticut law of 1703 called
for the flogging of any slaves caught in taverns without their
masters' permission.

THE WHISKEY REBELLION

The first truly American whiskey was distilled from
rye grain. It was produced in the frontier areas west of the
Appalachian Mountains in Maryland, Pennsylvania, and
Virginia. The farmers vastly preferred shipping the rye
whiskey rather than the actual rye grain over the mountains
to the markets in the eastern cities. The whiskey was much
less bulky and therefore less expensive to ship. Even George
Washington grew some rye at Mount Vernon and made
whiskey from it.

Victory in the revolutionary war left the newly established United States government heavily burdened with debt
and extremely short of cash. The young secretary of the treasury, Alexander Hamilton, sought to raise new revenues
through excise taxes. These were taxes on goods made in
America. In 1794 Hamilton levied one such tax on rye
whiskey.

The western farmers were outraged. They held turbu-
lent protest meetings, and pledged that they would never
pay one penny of the hated tax. Any federal revenue agents

seeking to collect it were roughly treated at the farmers' hands.

This so-called Whiskey Rebellion could have grown into a serious problem for the new government. It was the first test of federal authority by Americans. Would the young United States be forced to war against its own citizens?

President Washington sent a group of officials to try to reason with the rebels peaceably. When the envoys' efforts met with an angry and hostile reception, the president reluctantly ordered a detachment of militia to the area. The rebellion collapsed without a shot being fired, and federal authority was restored.

WHISKEY CONQUERS RUM

The excise tax on whiskey was repealed in 1802. Almost immediately whiskey surpassed rum in popularity, especially in the West. Corn for bourbon whiskey and rye grain for rye whiskey were available in virtually unlimited amounts, thus keeping the price down. A single bushel of surplus corn was enough to make three barrels of whiskey. And with the tax removed, whiskey now became much cheaper than rum.

British embargoes on rum exports and on molasses from the West Indies had helped make rum hard to get and therefore quite expensive during and immediately after the revolutionary war.

Technological improvements that made distilling more efficient contributed to increased sales of whiskey in the early nineteenth century. This was the first indication that the Industrial Revolution, already under way in Europe, would soon break out in America.

THE DRUNKARD'S PROGRESS.

4 EARLY SKIRMISHES: WETS VS. DRYS

(1800–1865)

4

A Surplus of Whiskey

At the start of the nineteenth century, the whiskey industry was mostly centered in the area between the Appalachian Mountains and the Mississippi River. So many distilleries had been built in upstate New York, western Pennsylvania, and Ohio that these regions were producing more than half the nation's spirits based on fruit or grain.

It was not long before these distilleries were producing more whiskey than the market could absorb. Inevitably, prices plummeted. The result of the overproduction of whiskey, along with that of agricultural commodities, was the Panic of 1819. This was the nation's first major economic crisis.

By the 1820s the West was in deep financial trouble. Westerners were accustomed to buying everything they needed in the big eastern cities. Their highly profitable whiskey sales had always made it easy to pay. But now they were producing a whiskey surplus, and the resulting tumble in prices sent their buying power cascading downward.

Some western farmers turned away from selling their whole output in the East. Instead they floated their grain

southward down the Ohio and Mississippi rivers to New
Orleans. From that point it was shipped to overseas markets.

At first they used rafts, flatboats, or keelboats as inexpensive freight carriers on the southward-flowing rivers.
They had to make the tedious, sometimes dangerous return
trip on foot, horseback, or expensive stagecoach.

Then, in 1807, Robert Fulton succeeded in navigating
his steamboat, the *Clermont,* upstream on the Hudson River.
The new invention was soon in use on the western water-
ways. The farmers' upriver return was now quick, easy, and
cheap.

Another result of the whiskey surplus was that many of
the small distilleries that had been built in the boom days
were unable to survive the collapse of whiskey prices. Fewer,
larger distilleries replaced them and now dominated the
industry.

After 1830 Americans gradually cut down on the huge
quantities they had been drinking. Ever-increasing numbers
preferred to invest their savings and disposable cash in the
new industrialization rapidly developing around them.
Many became accustomed, for the first time, to living without liquor. More than ever before were now employed in factories, where strict rules forbade drinking on the job.

By midcentury, however, many factory workers had
come to the realization that they were permanently stuck in
monotonous, dead-end jobs. Many turned to drink. Beer
drinking during this time registered a substantial increase.

THE "TEETOTAL" CONTROVERSY

The exact origins of the words *teetotal* and *teetotaler*
(one who totally abstains from drinking alcoholic beverages)
are uncertain.

One plausible story centers around the local temperance society in the small town of Hector, New York. In 1826 the society was torn by a lively debate as to whether its pledge cards should bind the signers to total abstinence, or allow them the option of abstaining only from distilled spirits (which would permit them to drink wine, beer, or hard cider).

The society decided to submit the matter to a referendum of the members. The names of those who voted in favor of total sobriety were marked with the letter *T* on the society's membership lists. They became known in the vicinity as "T-totalers." Other temperance societies adopted the term as they adopted total abstinence pledges, and the term *teetotaler* soon spread across the nation.

A national temperance convention met in Saratoga, New York, in 1836. It voted for total dryness as the only kind of temperance it recognized. At first some of the members resisted this as extreme and intolerant. But by 1840 teetotaling had won acceptance as the very meaning of temperance.

In 1855 the national temperance society reported that an estimated two million persons had given up distilled liquors. Their commitment had forced some four thousand distilleries to close. The society further reported that a quarter of a million persons had taken teetotal pledges.

Not surprisingly, liquor consumption fell off sharply during this period. In 1830 drinking had attained its greatest popularity, with an average of seven gallons of pure alcohol being drunk per capita annually. By 1840—within a single decade—per capita consumption had fallen to three gallons. This is the largest ten-year drop ever recorded in American history. The figure dropped even lower in the 1850s.

WAS DRINKING TRULY THE SOLE CAUSE?

In 1821 and again in 1824 well-researched studies of the causes of poverty were published in New York and Massachusetts. They concluded that excessive drinking was the principal cause of poverty. The author of a Maine report of the same era counted paupers in a local poorhouse. This researcher found that the vast majority had been reduced to poverty through heavy drinking by the heads of their households.

A contemporary survey of the penal system in the United States, published in a leading magazine, carried this line of opinion to the point of exaggeration. The author of this survey ignored the varied and complicated interaction of social factors. He stated with little evidence that hard liquor was "almost the sole cause of all the suffering, the poverty, and the crime to be found in this country."

In the early nineteenth century studies such as those discussed above gave single causes to explain a complicated problem like poverty. Modern sociologists have learned to be extremely cautious about such explanations. When they generalize about any large-scale social problem, they look for and usually find multiple causes. Nevertheless, these early nineteenth century studies did serve antiliquor forces as effective propaganda.

Later, in the 1880s, a nationwide survey was published that brought many of the prohibitionists' most firmly held beliefs into question.

A researcher had written to every "lunatic asylum" (as mental hospitals were termed at that time) in the United States. He asked them to provide a count of the patients of both sexes whose insanity had been diagnosed as the result of intemperance. The researcher then calculated the percent-age of the asylum's total population that had been so diagnosed.

Fifty-four institutions responded. On the basis of their figures the researcher concluded that the asylum doctors had found that just seven out of one hundred insanity cases were probably caused primarily by intemperance.

In an additional study of the causes of extreme poverty, the researcher used mainly the data of the 1875 Massachusetts census. Analysis of the data showed that alcohol abuse was either the effect, rather than the cause, or only one of the many causes of poverty.

As for crime, this researcher could only point out that many criminals used drunkenness as an excuse. The Germans drank a lot of beer, he noted, but seldom got drunk, went insane, became paupers, or committed crimes.

The temperance people proceeded as if no survey had ever been done. They clung to their unshakable belief that drunkenness was at least the main cause, if not the sole cause, of insanity, pauperism, and crime.

ORIGINS OF THE PROHIBITION MOVEMENT

Around 1818 a prominent New England preacher named Lyman Beecher joined the crusade against drinking. The force and power of his eloquence impelled thousands to sign abstinence pledges.

It was a time when America's easygoing tolerance for drinking was beginning to erode. Employers and farmers stopped paying their workmen partly in liquor. On the railroads any mistake committed by an employee who had been drinking might cost many lives. The railroads therefore began to fire people caught drinking at work.

The U.S. Army abolished the liquor ration formerly allotted to the troops. No alcoholic beverage of any kind could henceforth be sold on any military base.

The distinguished Senator Henry Clay of Kentucky gave a series of formal dinner parties, all widely publicized, at which no alcoholic drinks were served.

In 1828, Beecher and a group of Bostonians founded the first national temperance society, the American Society for the Promotion of Temperance (which later became the American Temperance Union). Eventually it boasted five thousand chapters.

This organization was the first to adopt the total banning of all intoxicating beverages as its goal. Not all of its members favored such a radical proposal, and many resigned.

The Prohibition movement brought other kinds of opposition into being. As long as the temperance movement concentrated its fire on distilled liquors, the beer brewers had strongly supported it. But now the movement had declared war on all alcoholic beverages. The brewers joined forces with the distillers, financing wet candidates and sometimes bribing political officeholders to back wet causes.

THE STRESSES AND STRAINS OF CHANGE

The 1820s and 1830s witnessed the development of an immensely popular religious revival movement, sometimes termed "The Second Great Awakening." The first "Great Awakening" had swept the country in a revival of evangelical fervor in the mideighteenth century. In both "awakenings," preachers roamed the land, delivering passionate sermons against sin—and against drinking—to vast, enthusiastic crowds. Many of these clergymen expounded a simple fundamentalist faith.

The temperance movement could hardly help being influenced by this evangelical revival. A high percentage of temperance leaders were clergymen. Fundamentalism helped breed an uncompromising version of temperance.

No longer was it enough to speak out in favor of moderation in drinking. Temperance advocates now began to insist on total abstinence as the only truly worthy goal of their movement. The new preaching evoked nationwide enthusiasm.

The reasons for this warm reception were rooted in the way many Americans felt about the sweeping changes taking place in the United States. The country was in the throes of social and economic upheaval. People from small towns and rural areas were feeling displaced and disoriented in the new industrializing America that was brutally shouldering its way into existence around them. These people yearned for the older, gentler, more orderly way of life they fondly remembered.

They felt hemmed in by the explosive growth of the American population. It was doubling every twenty-three years. They resented the waves of immigrants, the ceaseless surge of westward migrations, the dynamic expansion of the cities, and the transformation of many farm laborers into factory workers with fading memories, if any, of life close to the soil.

Farm workers had once been able to aspire realistically to save enough to become landowning farmers themselves. This dream was now becoming a practical impossibility for most.

Nor were the workers much more contented in the factories. They worked long hours, six days a week, for low wages. Working conditions were often deplorable. Drinking was an easy outlet for many.

Cheap and abundant liquor was increasingly available to the poorest classes. Unbridled drinking resulted in what nondrinking citizens perceived as the ugliness and disorder marring the American way of life they had once known and loved.

They liked and understood the simple, uncomplicated feelings expressed in T. S. Arthur's best-selling book of 1854, *Ten Nights in a Barroom and What I Saw There*. In 1858 William Pratt turned the book into a hugely popular play. Its tear-jerking climax comes when little Mary stands pitiably at the saloon door and sings the familiar ballad, "Father, Dear Father, Come Home with Me Now."

Even more successful was W. H. Smith's play, *The Drunkard or the Fallen Saved*. First produced in 1844, it broke all records for popularity. The simple, sentimental play, with its warning against the evils of drink, is still a hit whenever it is staged today. It recently ran for nine years in a Los Angeles revival.

Students were different, too. By the 1840s they had become notorious for their heavy drinking more than their traditional appetite for learning.

Still another disturbing change was making itself felt. In the early nineteenth century new classes of workmen came into being. Their jobs kept them on the move around the country. They included stagecoach drivers and riverboat pilots, lumbermen, and canal builders. Most of these men were rootless, without families or social ties. Another thing they seemed to have in common was that they consumed tremendous quantities of liquor.

WINE FOR THE UPPER CLASSES

Until about 1825 wine was mostly favored by the upper classes, who could afford it. Being an imported product, it cost much more than whiskey. Patriotic Americans were critical of wine drinkers, who favored this expensive foreign product over good, inexpensive, American-made whiskey. Besides, the purchase of wine worsened America's unfavorable balance of imports over exports.

In response to these criticisms, groups of wine drinkers sponsored the planting of American wine grapes. Thomas Jefferson was among those who approved an experiment in 1805 in which Swiss vintners planted grapevines. Like all the other trial plantings of these sensitive plants, the experiment failed.

Wine drinking decreased by about half after 1840, largely because more and more people were giving up all use of liquor and turning to abstinence.

SOME ODD EFFECTS OF DRINKING ON POLITICS

Andrew Jackson was a popular soldier-hero when he was elected president in 1828. Huge crowds of friends and well-wishers turned up at his inauguration gala the following March. The host provided almost limitless amounts of liquor. So rowdy did the crowd become that they had to be moved out of the White House lest the building suffer damage. But how could such a drunken mob be moved? A member of Jackson's staff came up with the simple answer. Move the liquor to the lawn outside, and the people would follow. They did, and the White House was saved from harm.

William Henry Harrison ran for president in 1840. In an article published by his opponents, they alleged that the elderly Harrison would do better to stay home in a log cabin with a jug.

Harrison's campaign managers seized upon this image as one that the common man would surely enjoy. The log cabin was used throughout the country, and the Harrison people made sure that thousands of little jugs of hard cider were passed out to the voters. Harrison won by a large margin.

In the ensuing years many a politician running for office presented himself as a humble "log cabin candidate," even if he was really born and raised in a marble mansion and drank his liquor out of a golden cup rather than a jug.

DRINKING ON THE FRONTIER

By the 1830s and 1840s the ever-moving western frontier of the United States had reached the trans-Appalachian region but had not yet crossed the Mississippi.

White men first penetrated the wilderness west of the Mississippi around the time of the Civil War (1861–1865). Leading the way was a wild and motley crew of adventurers. They included fur trappers (often living solitary lives in the hills, and known as "mountain men"), prospectors searching for precious metals, cowboys, and detachments of the U.S. Army. When they could get it, these men drank great quantities of whiskey.

Some of them often lived for weeks, even months, far from human society and the comforts of civilization. Often they made arrangements to come together more or less regularly, partly to do business, partly to enjoy several days of uninhibited good times. The most famous meetings were the so-called "rendezvous," at which the mountain men met twice a year to trade their furs and whoop it up.

As for cowboys, the typical behavior pattern showed itself when they arrived at some town after long weeks of herding cattle out on the hot, dusty prairie. Many tended to spend their wages all too quickly on alcohol.

Many frontiersmen nurtured beliefs about certain supposed powers of whiskey. One of the most common superstitions was that whiskey was an effective antidote for snakebite. Believers prescribed a full quart of whiskey, to be drunk within twelve hours. The victim would certainly be affected; he would get very drunk first and sometimes even die.

Other beliefs were based on truth. Whiskey was sometimes used as an anti-infection agent that was poured over an area of the body just before it underwent surgery. The alcohol in the whiskey probably did have some germicidal effect, though those who used whiskey for this purpose undoubtedly did not understand the benefits of alcohol.

Before the discovery of ether, whiskey was also used on the frontier (and by many city doctors as well) as an anesthetic during surgery. The patient, having been fed copious quantities, would unquestionably suffer less. But it is doubtful that any patient ever attained the state of pain-free unconsciousness produced by modern anesthetics.

Without a doubt frontiersmen were rough, hard-drinking men, and whether they were conscious of it or not they comprised the vanguard of the westward-moving nation.

The Washingtonians

In 1840, in Baltimore, a group of six self-admitted drunkards were discussing their drinking habit. It was ruining their lives, they concluded. They made up their minds to found a new temperance society. In honor of George Washington (despite his being a drinker), they named it the Washington Temperance Society.

As a token of their earnest wish to reform, they all signed pledges of total abstinence. They decided that their society would be different from the existing ones. First of all, they decided to make it nonreligious. Instead of seeking to improve society at large, or to have laws passed to place limits on drinking or to ban it altogether, they would focus on the individual alcoholic. They resolved to make no distinctions among the alcoholics they would work with: rich or poor, respectable or disreputable, churchgoing or not, longtime drunks or new drinkers, apparently incurable cases or easy ones.

The Washingtonians, as they came to be called, succeeded beyond their fondest expectations. Within a few months more than a thousand drinkers had signed abstinence pledges. Branches of the Washingtonian movement were quickly formed in many cities.

Help offered by the Washingtonians included their trying to find a job for any ex-drunk who needed one, or their giving temporary financial aid to the reformed drinkers. The Washingtonians were convinced that ex-drunks needed to change their lifestyles completely. They must avoid their former drinking haunts and the ever-present demons of temptation.

The Washingtonians introduced a feature at their meetings that had never been tried before. Reformed drunks were invited to address the meetings, telling in vivid and often painful detail about their ruinous experiences under the influence of alcohol. They told how their lives and careers, as well as their families' lives, had suffered.

One result was that large numbers of sympathetic men in the audience, many of them openly moved to tears, signed abstinence pledges. Today, such self-revelations are a regular feature at meetings of Alcoholics Anonymous.

With the Washingtonians' assistance, an estimated total of about 600,000 drunks had pledged to reform within a relatively short time. Ultimately, about 150,000 of these never drank again; the rest relapsed at least to some extent. No other temperance movement could boast such a record of success.

Surprisingly, the Washingtonian movement faded away almost as fast as it had risen to such heights of popularity. It had neither a long-range objective nor any central governing body. The churches and the established temperance societies, which had been allies at first, withdrew their support. There was no single or direct cause for the Washingtonians' demise, but by 1847 virtually all local branches had stopped meeting.

THE FIRST STATEWIDE PROHIBITION LAW

One of the most determined crusaders for Prohibition was a Maine man named Neal Dow. He was firmly convinced that the well-being and the very life of the republic were endangered by the easy availability of liquor. It was the root cause of a long list of social evils, he believed, and a threat to the stability of the family.

Dow was certain that the surest way to protect the people of Maine was through the passage of a state law prohibiting the manufacture, distribution, and sale of alcohol for drinking purposes.

He was tireless in his efforts to get such a law enacted. Throughout the mid-1840s he carried his message from one end of the state to the other. He pleaded with politicians,

helped get local restrictions on liquor sales passed, and col-
lected thousands of signatures on a Prohibition petition.
More than once he faced the threat of physical violence from
the enemies of Prohibition.

Dow's campaign came to a victorious conclusion in 1851
with the enactment of the Maine Law. He could rest assured
that it was a thorough and effective Prohibition statute,
because he had written it himself. It is true that Massachusetts
had passed a law back in 1838 banning retail sales of distilled spirits, but popular resistance was so strong that it was
quickly repealed. The Maine Law lasted much longer.

The year 1851 also saw Dow elected mayor of Portland,
Maine's largest city. While in office he took special pleasure
in enforcing the new antiliquor law rigorously, even enthusi-
astically.

By 1855 twelve other states and two provinces of
Canada had passed Prohibition laws based upon the Maine
Law. Prohibition had become the second most talked about,
most popular cause in the years before the Civil War. The
abolition of slavery was the one cause discussed more
widely, and more passionately.

DRY IRISH CATHOLICS

The Irish constituted the largest single wave of
immigrants to enter the U.S. in the decades preceding the
Civil War. Two million had immigrated by 1860. The pota-
to crop, Ireland's main food source, failed for several years
starting in 1848. Famine struck Ireland, and a large part of
the desperate population had no choice but to emigrate from
their beloved homeland to America.

Here they received anything but a warm welcome. The
Irish were almost all Roman Catholic, and there was a good

deal of prejudice against them among the mostly Protestant population of the United States.

In 1850 a group of extreme American nationalists founded the American Party (popularly called the Know-Nothings, because of their practice of secrecy). Its chief aim was to shield the republic from destruction by immigrants dedicated to a foreign and supposedly antirepublican faith (Roman Catholicism).

The Irish soon found that only the lowest-paying, most undesirable jobs were open to them. Many could find no job at all. Many Help Wanted ads in the newspapers carried the warning, "No Irish Need Apply."

Oppressed by such treatment, and facing the grim reality of abject poverty, many Irishmen turned to liquor for at least a temporary escape from their woes. Drinking was no new thing for the Irish, as it was an accepted part of life in the old country. Drunkenness there was common enough to be considered a serious social problem.

A priest in Ireland, Father Theobald Matthew, who believed in abstinence as the only solution to the drinking habit, had established a highly successful Catholic Total Abstinence League. He emigrated to the United States in 1849. When Father Theobald proposed to set up an American branch of his organization, he received a favorable response from many thousands of the Catholic immigrants.

Nevertheless, the temperance movement continued to be dominated by the Protestants.

THE GERMAN IMMIGRATION AND LAGER BEER

During the same years that witnessed the high tide of Irish immigration, Germans also began to flock into this country. Almost a million had arrived by 1860, and three million by 1900. They generally were accepted into the American population more easily and successfully than the Irish. The Germans had an unusually high proportion of well-educated people among them. Many had enough capital to start their own businesses.

The Germans also brought old drinking habits with them. Beer had long been their favorite beverage, beer of a special kind called lager beer. The finest lager was brewed from water, hops, and malt.

Lager means "to ripen." The beer was allowed to age or ripen longer than American brews. Aging gave it a mellower flavor. Almost all lager beer in this country was the product of immigrant German brew masters.

The new beer quickly won the favor of native-born Americans, with one exception. They tended to drink more and faster than the Germans, and therefore preferred their beer to be somewhat lighter and colder than the traditional German lager. The ultimate result was the light beer Americans still enjoy today.

Distribution of beer in America's vast spaces was a problem. Beer barrels and kegs were bulky, heavy, and expensive to ship over long distances. The solution was local, family-owned breweries. By midcentury these were a common sight in many American towns and cities.

Despite their fondness for beer, the Germans never were identified with drunkenness. They had no such tradition in Germany. Their quick and easy integration into American society eliminated any need to rely on liquor as an escape mechanism.

HORACE MANN TRIES TO HELP

Horace Mann was a distinguished Massachusetts-born educator. He was also an ardent temperance advocate. Mann saw that farmers made up a majority in the American population of the first half of the nineteenth century. Most were drinkers. If they could somehow be turned into abstainers, that would constitute a great victory for temperance. How could he approach them most effectively?

The farmers' main sources of liquor were the rural grocers. Mann wrote a forceful pamphlet aimed not at the farmers but at the grocers. They must stop selling liquor to the farmers, he wrote. Drinking only reduced productivity and profits on the farms. Farmers with less to show at the end of the year in the way of profit were less valuable to the grocers as customers.

Surprising to Mann, this closely reasoned and well-written pamphlet, backed up by the authority of one of the nation's most respected educators, was not nearly as effective as Mann and his supporters had hoped it would be.

Mann had overlooked one fact: Liquor sales were the biggest profit makers the grocers had. Naturally, they were reluctant to give up these profits.

THE IMPACT OF THE CIVIL WAR (1861–1865)

Even the devastating four-year Civil War did not put a halt to temperance activities. Local societies kept up the struggle, as did the nationwide American Temperance Union. The war, however, absorbed the nation's attention and virtually all its energies. The temperance forces were unable to achieve any major breakthroughs during the war years.

With so many men off fighting the war, there was considerably less drinking at home and in taverns. The soldiers in the opposing American armies behaved as troops in all armies have behaved since time immemorial: They drank quite heavily whenever and wherever they could get liquor. No regular liquor ration was provided to the troops of either side.

There were a few military units, however, that practiced temperance. Some Northern regiments even organized their own temperance societies.

Maine's Neal Dow rose to the rank of general. He recruited several Maine regiments, and personally saw to it that all their troops took the pledge of temperance.

The temperance movement's greatest days lay ahead. The most important factor in its renewed growth and vitality was the tremendous swelling of its ranks by the sector of the population that had the most to gain from the triumph of temperance: American women.

5 WOMEN JOIN THE BATTLE

(1860–1900)

5

THE CIVIL WAR AND THE POSTWAR YEARS

When the Civil War broke out in 1861, Abraham Lincoln and his colleagues faced a dire shortage of money to pay for it. New taxes would obviously be needed. Prime targets were the giant distilling and brewing industries. Fortunately for the government, neither had yet organized a central body that might have protested. There was little opposition as both were subjected to new taxation under the 1861 Civil War tax legislation.

To the astonishment of the authorities, totally unexpected opposition was then expressed by the drys. They objected to the new taxes because they felt that taxation of any activity implied legitimization or government approval of it. Since liquor was inherently evil, the government ought to tax it no more than it would tax crime.

But the government needed the added revenues so badly that the bill passed anyway. One immediate result was that the formerly unorganized brewers formed the United States Brewers Association to defend their interests.

The flourishing Prohibition movement all but vanished from public consciousness during the war. The country's attention was riveted on the great military duel between the Union and the Confederacy. No other cause could occupy the public mind while the fateful battle went on.

Temperance and Prohibition leaders tried in the years immediately after the war to persuade the Republican and Democratic parties to join their cause. The response was disappointing. As a result, the prohibitionists tried to launch Prohibition parties in several states. Finally, in 1869, temperance leaders held a national convention at which they founded a National Prohibition party.

The new party nominated its first presidential candidate, James Black, in 1872. He tallied only a little more than five thousand votes. Still, the prohibitionists had at least proven that they were active in the field. They might well become a force to be reckoned with in the future. Just as the abolitionists had rid the land of the curse of human slavery, the prohibitionists pledged to rid it of the curse of alcoholic slavery.

The Prohibition party never became the powerful political force that its supporters hoped for. Some other form of organization would have to be found to lead the charge against drinking.

AN UNAPPETIZING DIET

The food Americans ate had a great deal to do with the quantities of alcohol they drank. Dominated by corn, their meals were monotonous and tasteless. Average Americans are thought to have consumed a pound of bread a day. It was almost always made from cornmeal. Along with it went a pound of meat, usually salt pork.

Americans ate more meat than did the people of any

other nation. With the country still only sparsely settled, beef cattle were allowed to graze on the open and unfenced range, at no cost. Meat was therefore quite inexpensive.

Since ovens were not yet common, meats could neither be roasted nor baked. Boiling and frying were the only alternatives. Strong drink seemed the only acceptable accompaniment to this fatty, greasy, unwholesome diet.

THE WOMAN'S CHRISTIAN TEMPERANCE UNION

The organization that developed into the largest and most powerful force in the temperance movement, the Woman's Christian Temperance Union, was founded in Cleveland, Ohio, in 1874. Its charter members included women from seventeen states. It stood for temperance, morality, and women's rights.

The founding and activation of the WCTU also marked the first time large numbers of American women had ever entered into politics and social action.

For many years the WCTU conducted a successful nationwide campaign to get temperance literature into the schools. The union's aim was to make temperance and an understanding of the dangers of drinking an important part of every child's education. At the WCTU's urging, numerous major magazines banned liquor advertising and printed temperance editorials.

The WCTU's leaders denounced society's tolerant attitude toward cheap, abundant liquor as one of the true causes of drunkenness. Blame should not be directed at the individual drunkard, whom the WCTU supporters viewed as needing help and understanding. Accordingly, the

WCTU's energies were devoted primarily to the reformation of individual alcoholics, and only secondarily to political action on behalf of antiliquor laws.

The WCTU's chief means of converting heavy drinkers became known as "gospel temperance." This was a blending of religion and antidrinking persuasion aimed first at kindling some spark of godliness within the drinker. Secondarily the WCTU women tried to get the drinker to sign—and stick to—a pledge of total abstinence.

The WCTU was later able to claim accurately that gospel temperance had proven highly effective. Thousands of drunkards had been converted. Relapses, or returns to drinking, had been prevented by the formation of "Reform Clubs." These were self-governing groups of alcoholics and problem drinkers who banded together to help one another to remain sober.

The WCTU's work with drunkards was in the tradition of the Washingtonians of the 1840s, and in many ways foreshadowed today's Alcoholics Anonymous.

THE SPECIAL PROBLEMS OF FEMALE ALCOHOLICS

Though men constituted the vast majority of heavy drinkers, a substantial number of women, too, were addicted to alcohol. Their number, during this time, has been estimated at around 100,000. The proportion of women alcoholics among all drunks has been placed somewhere between one out of ten and one out of three.

Some women were "innocent" drinkers. They purchased and drank the many patent medicines that then flooded the marketplace. These concoctions were advertised as remedies

for every type of ailment. In actuality they were rarely effective medicinally. Many contained high percentages of alcohol. In those years manufacturers were not required to list
the ingredients of their products on the labels. Women who
habitually used these patent medicines often became alcoholics without realizing it.

Through most of the nineteenth century, it was far more
disastrous for a woman to be branded with the stigma of
alcoholism than for a man. This double standard reflected
the puritanical male-dominated morality of mid- and late-
nineteenth-century America.

Women were thought of as "the weaker sex," and their
proper place was in the home. There they reigned by dint of
their superior virtue and strict morality. Respectable women
might be permitted an occasional glass of sherry, but supposedly they seldom touched any liquor beyond that one
drink.

Women alcoholics were regarded as abnormal. They had
forsaken hearth and home and abandoned the standards of
acceptable behavior. They were "debauched" women, and
could not be received as guests in any proper household.

Women who had a drinking problem but wished to
remain acceptable in respectable society had to resort to
secrecy and "hidden" drinking. A highly placed officer of the
WCTU declared in 1876 that "half the ladies of wealth and
fashion" regularly "disguised" their drinking to avoid social
ostracism.

One result was that by the time female alcoholics sought
medical help, they probably had been concealing their
condition so long that it had become untreatable. Most
nineteenth-century doctors believed that women alcoholics
could not be rehabilitated as readily as men. Alcohol-caused

medical complications were thought to be more severe in women. Deaths due to alcoholism were more than twice as common in women as in men.

At its very first convention in 1874, the WCTU called for the construction of sanitariums for female alcoholics at local, state, and federal expense. No public funding was ever voted for this purpose.

One such institution, the privately financed Temple Home, was established in Binghamton, New York, in 1876. It is thought to have flourished for only a few years. Another, the so-called Women's National Hospital, also funded from private sources, was opened in Connecticut in 1874 for alcoholics and opium addicts. It remained open until 1885. Society's attitudes toward women were not yet sufficiently developed to admit that female alcoholism, and female opium addiction as well, were major social problems urgently demanding attention.

THE DOCTORS' DEBATE

Doctors were sharply divided as to whether alcohol was a poisonous substance or could be used safely and effectively for medical purposes. The issue was debated endlessly throughout the nineteenth century. It was not settled until the early 1900s, when the American Medical Association yielded to pressure from militant temperance groups and declared alcohol unacceptable in any form or mixture for medicinal use.

Other questions that aroused interest among medical men included the kinds of medical treatment that should be administered to alcoholics and how alcoholism could be studied scientifically.

The idea that alcohol addiction was a disease had been winning acceptance among ever-growing numbers of physicians as early as the late eighteenth century. The idea had since spread to many temperance workers.

If alcoholism was truly a disease, the next logical step was to build asylums or sanitariums for drunkards. Alcoholics needed specialized professional help, which would be available only in such facilities.

In the years leading up to the Civil War, the campaign for asylums was led by Dr. Joseph E. Turner of Maine. He contended that asylums would not only have the newest and best treatment available, but would also make it possible for medical researchers to study large numbers of alcoholics under controlled conditions. Major advances in the scientific understanding of alcoholism would undoubtedly emerge from these studies.

THE "KEELEY CURE"

In 1880 Dr. Leslie Keeley of Illinois made a startling announcement. He claimed he had discovered a medicine that cured alcoholism and drug addiction. Keeley then proceeded to establish a Keeley Institute at Dwight, Illinois. Losing no time, he began treating patients at once.

Keeley's work attracted no major publicity until 1891, when the *Chicago Tribune* published a series of articles praising it in glowing terms. Alcoholics and drug addicts soon were flocking to Dwight. During the 1890s Keeley took advantage of his newfound fame to open branch institutes all over the country. By 1900 every state had at least one Keeley Institute; some had as many as three.

Keeley said the secret miracle ingredient in his remedy

was "Bichloride of Gold" or "Double Chloride of Gold." The medicine was popularly known as the "Gold Cure." The substance he had named was unknown to pharmacologists, and Keeley obdurately refused to reveal his formula. Most probably it was some sort of gold salt, mixed with an assortment of vegetable compounds.

Several similar medicines, also based on gold, were marketed in the 1880s. Unlike Keeley, some of his competitors were unafraid to publicize their formulae.

Keeley soon had to deal with more serious troubles. Physicians all over the country specializing in alcoholism publicly denounced him as a quack. Keeley insisted that the surest method of administering the Keeley Cure was to inject the medicine intravenously at one of his institutes.

Keeley was a shrewd and aggressive businessman. Calling his former patients "graduates," he appointed many of them to serve as "missionaries" for his cure. He even set up a "Keeley League" of ex-patients, which held yearly conventions and hired lecturers to speak on behalf of the Keeley Cure.

According to one estimate, about 400,000 persons had taken the cure by 1918. By then, however, its popularity was waning. Keeley died in 1900. Many of his former patients relapsed into drunkenness fairly soon after taking the alleged cure, casting doubt on its efficacy. Public charges by other physicians that Keeley's practices made no scientific sense further diminished the cure's appeal.

By the 1920s only eleven institutes were still functioning. In time, all but the institute at Dwight either closed or dissociated themselves from the cure. Even the Dwight branch, though it still exists today, makes no claim to cure drunkenness.

The Gold Cure was almost certainly a fraud, but its years of amazing success were undoubtedly due, in part at least, to the fact that no more effective remedy was available at the time.

THE "NEW IMMIGRANTS"

During the 1880s floods of immigrants kept coming to the United States, but gradually their countries of origin began to change. At first there were still plenty of Irish and Germans, along with many other northern Europeans. But by 1900 the overwhelming majority came from southern, eastern, and central Europe. They were termed the "new immigrants." So many poured in that the number of foreign-born rose from about 4 million in 1860 to roughly 13.5 million in 1910.

For the first time, a large proportion were Jews and Italians. They were accustomed to drinking in their home countries. There they had limited their drinking to mealtimes and special occasions such as weddings, funerals, certain religious ceremonies, and holidays.

The two groups were also similar in that they had the same intolerant attitude toward drunkenness. Of all immigrant groups in America, they ranked among the lowest in their rates of alcoholism.

Meanwhile, the temperance movement was quietly gathering strength for an all-out assault on drinking. Its greatest victory was still in the future, but it was closer than either wets or drys could imagine.

6 THE COMING OF PROHIBITION

(1870–1917)

(previous page)
New York City's Hoffman
House Bar, illustrated here
about 1890, was a saloon
frequented by an upper-
class clientele.
(Library of Congress)

6

.
.
.
.
.
.
.
.
.
.
.

DRYS ON THE MARCH

.
.
.

Prohibition laws had been passed by several states before the Civil War. They had been unpopular and, in some cases, unenforceable. Within a few years of their enactment, virtually all were repealed.

But in the 1870s and 1880s, the prohibitionists found new grounds for hope in Kansas. That state's Republican governor, John St. John, was a fighting reformer and prohibitionist. With the active support of the Woman's Christian Temperance Union, he won two hard-fought election battles in the 1870s. While in office he pushed the first Prohibition law since the Civil War through to passage.

Led by the Anti-Saloon League, the fight spread rapidly to other states. Mothers carried their young children with them as they entreated legislators for dry laws as protection of their homes and children.

Four more states passed Prohibition laws in the 1880s: North and South Dakota, Iowa, and Rhode Island. Georgia followed suit in 1907. By 1913, forty-six million people, or half the population, were living under some form of prohibitory law.

Also in 1913 the Webb-Kenyon Act was passed. Under its terms no liquor could be shipped from wet states to dry ones. A severe blow to the liquor interests, it was a clear signal of tougher laws to come.

The battle was fought out across the country; in many states the wets prevented dry victories only by marshaling last-ditch resistance. But it was clear that the drys were gaining ground.

A formidable obstacle facing the drys was the anti-Prohibition stance adopted by the two major parties. Both the Democratic and Republican parties included wets and drys. Each refused to risk intraparty squabbles over Prohibition that might endanger party unity.

In the election campaign of 1884 the Republicans learned how sensitive an issue drinking was. Their presidential candidate was James G. Blaine, who was accused of being corrupt and was certainly a wet. He was running against Grover Cleveland.

In a speech made in New York City at the height of the campaign, one of Blaine's chief aides denounced the Democratic party as the party of "Rum, Romanism, and Rebellion." Part of his audience was Irish and, of course, Roman Catholic. The speaker had thoughtlessly insulted both their religion and their drinking.

The Irish vote formed a significant bloc in the New York electorate. Formerly expected to go heavily Republican, the Irish vote went solidly for Cleveland and the Democrats. Blaine lost New York's electoral votes and the election. The defeat was partly because the Prohibition party won several thousand New York votes he badly needed, and partly because of his aide's gratuitous insult to the Irish.

A fourth national party, the Populist party, was formed

in 1890. It, too, proved inhospitable to the prohibitionists' pleas. Like the Democrats and Republicans, the Populist membership was too divided on the Prohibition issue for the party to take a clear stand one way or the other.

THE ANTI-SALOON LEAGUE

The Anti-Saloon League was originally an offshoot of the WCTU, though it admitted men as well as women. The league was founded in 1893 to enable the WCTU and other antiliquor forces to take active roles in partisan politics without offending the Democratic or Republican parties. It supported candidates who favored Prohibition, whether they were Democrats or Republicans.

The league also supported the principle of "local option," under which a town or a county could vote itself dry even if the rest of the state was wet.

By proving that it could line up its voters to back any candidate it supported, the league won the respect of both major parties. It made a reliable supply of campaign workers available to help candidates favorable to temperance, and supported such candidates with financial donations.

In 1913 the league announced that its ultimate goal was national Prohibition. The following year a league-sponsored Prohibition bill was defeated in Congress, but twenty-four states already had Prohibition laws.

The league also had the American Issues Press at its disposal. It published a vast amount of league propaganda, keeping its members well armed with sound protemperance and antisaloon arguments.

At the same time, the league lived up to its name. In accordance with its slogan The Saloon Must Go! it waged a relentless campaign to close down as many saloons as it could. This was no easy task.

The cities were dotted with opulently furnished saloons catering to affluent American-born members of high society. Many were located in the country's oldest and finest hotels, such as New York's Fifth Avenue Hotel, San Francisco's Palace, and Chicago's Palmer House. Some posh bars operated as parts of famous restaurants, such as Delmonico's in New York.

Far more numerous were the many smaller saloons frequented by middle-class patrons. They were often as lavishly decorated as the bigger places. Their clientele sometimes developed genuine affection for these more intimate establishments. Some even wrote sentimental memoirs about them.

Drunken or rowdy behavior was not tolerated in the saloons. The patrons came to relax, to enjoy the company of good friends, and to have a quiet good time.

The prohibitionists remained stubbornly convinced that moderate drinking (whether in saloons or at home) led inevitably to problem drinking and alcoholism. Citizens under the influence were potential threats to civic peace, the status of women, and the stability of the republic. The pleasant surroundings of the saloons only heightened the devilish temptation to drink.

One can imagine the ladies of the WCTU and the Anti-Saloon Leaguers invading these peaceful locales to hold their earnest sessions of prayer and hymn singing. Thoroughly annoyed drinkers were their involuntary audience. Though most saloon keepers did not conceal their anger at the temperance people's repeated appearances and their fervent entreaties to close up shop, it is a surprising fact that some did shut down.

By the turn of the century the league had added so many new chapters and so many dues-paying members that its annual budget rose to $2 million. Fully 80 percent of that sum came from donations of less than $100, evidence of the league's grassroots base.

Many reform-minded Catholics joined the Protestant-led league. A number of priests were among them; some rose to high office in the league. The turn of the century was a time of many reform movements: for improved education, for woman suffrage, for a progressive income tax, and for the direct election of senators, for instance. These reforms are usually grouped together under the term "social gospel," reflecting their blend of social action with religious inspiration. For Catholics as well as Protestants, the fight for Prohibition was one of the most sacred causes.

SALOON BUSINESS

Some saloons had profitable ties with organized prostitution. This was true, for example, of nearly half the 8,037 saloons that Philadelphia boasted in 1876. It was a logical and inevitable connection. Drinking men seeking good times often came to the saloons for more than drinks.

Many saloons were owned by breweries. They sold their owners' beer. Sales competition was fierce among the breweries, which naturally did everything possible to promote heavy drinking.

One popular technique to stimulate drinking was for a bartender to start things off by buying a round of free drinks for everyone. The hope was that customers would follow suit. It usually worked. The customers who bought the free rounds felt that they were demonstrating to all and sundry that they could afford the treat. Payday was the best day to get the workers to buy rounds.

Another stimulant to drinking was the "free lunch." It was customarily salted abundantly to inspire thirst, and was guarded by sharp-eyed "bouncers." These burly men saw to it that anyone who tried to avail himself of too much free lunch was promptly and roughly deposited on the sidewalk outside.

New customers also got free drinks. Saloon keepers even gave free drinks to young boys. They would undoubtedly pay the money back many times over when they grew to drinking age.

During the years from about 1870 to 1920 the saloon came to play a central role in workingmen's lives. It was a home away from home, offering food, drink, shelter, and one other highly valued amenity not usually available at home: companionship.

It evolved into a headquarters for a wide range of other activities. Many a labor union was born from saloon discussions. Political events were also the subject of lively debate. Immigrants needing advice or assistance could usually find it there, drawing upon the knowledgeable bartender's lore or upon some fellow customer's expertise.

LOBBYING AGAINST SALOONS

Around the turn of the century an Ohio citizen named Wayne B. Wheeler was named director of the Anti-Saloon League's campaign for national dry laws. Wheeler was a firm believer in the league's glorious destiny: to purify and exalt America.

Wheeler was no newcomer to politics. He had already

organized and led the league's first significant victory, the triumphant local option drive that dried up Ohio and other parts of the country. In 1905 he marshaled league votes solidly behind the dry Democratic candidate for governor, and defeated the wet Republican incumbent. Yet Wheeler himself was a Republican.

He subsequently became the league's general counsel in Washington. When any lawmaker showed signs of vacillating on dry legislation, Wheeler reminded him of the league's strength by seeing to it that the lawmaker's office was constantly crowded with prohibitionist lobbyists, and that the lawmaker was flooded with pro-dry telegrams.

Wheeler made the league the most feared and respected pressure group of the era. Proliquor spokesmen, such as the eloquent George Coes Howell, denounced what they considered the prohibitionists' "ignorant emotionalism." In an indirect reference to Wheeler, they said the prohibitionist drive was "directed by brilliant fanatics."

PROHIBITION AND SOCIAL REFORM

Reformers felt that the drive for temperance was an important weapon in the struggle against many social evils, especially poverty. Drinking was believed to be the cause of destitution in at least 20 percent of all urban poverty cases.

The spread of "skid rows" in many cities and towns (skid row is the district in any town inhabited by homeless poor people, most of whom are usually thought to be alcoholic) was often cited as further evidence of the link between liquor and poverty.

The inhabitants of skid row—generally termed "skid

row bums"— have unfortunately come to be stereotyped as hopeless drunks. But almost a century later, in the 1980s, sociological research showed that most skid row residents were not alcoholics. Furthermore, the percentage of the nation's alcoholics living on skid rows was found to be probably under 3 or 4 percent.

Temperance and the antisaloon campaign also helped in the fight against political corruption, which was then rampant in the big cities. Many saloons were designated as polling places. That did not prevent corrupt politicians from using these same saloons as their headquarters.

The saloons' regular customers could earn free drinks or a little cash by stuffing ballot boxes with fraudulent votes. Brawny customers intimidated the opposing party's voters and kept them from voting.

On the side of reform and Prohibition, medical science joined the fray. The doctors warned ever more insistently about the physical and mental dangers of liquor.

Some of the nation's leading industrialists, ever in need of sober and dependable workmen, spoke out in favor of Prohibition. Among them were John D. Rockefeller and Henry Ford. The very first entry in steel tycoon Andrew Carnegie's "Advice to Young Men" warned "never to enter a bar-room, nor let the contents of a bar-room enter you."

At the opposite end of the social scale, working-class customers began to desert the saloons that had once been centers of their leisure-time lives. Many of the workers' fraternal organizations and unions had their earliest beginnings in the saloons for want of any other affordable meeting place. The saloon keepers were only too glad to host such meetings.

But now that they had evolved into large and powerful

entities, their leaders separated them from the saloons and headquartered them in more respectable locations.

It was thus becoming increasingly apparent that an informal majority favoring Prohibition had formed across the United States, though no one had as yet attempted an accurate count. An influential political magazine, *The Nation,* and the coast-to-coast chain of newspapers run by William Randolph Hearst, added their powerful voices. Novelist Jack London, then at the height of his fame (and notwithstanding his own heavy drinking), argued for Prohibition for the sake of future generations.

National Prohibition could not be held off for long.

STEP BY STEP

The Anti-Saloon League had a foretaste of the coming victory in 1914. As usual it backed all congressional candidates favoring Prohibition. In greater numbers than ever, these drys won election. So many more drys were elected to the House and Senate in 1916 that the passage of a Prohibition law was virtually certain.

The following year the United States joined the Allies in World War I. In the effort to mobilize every aspect of the country's economic life, Congress passed a number of laws regulating the food supply. Using the pretext that it would save grain, the drys tacked an amendment onto one of these laws, forbidding the use of grain for the manufacture of alcoholic beverages.

More suddenly, more swiftly, and more easily than had ever been anticipated, the United States had taken the first portentous step toward national Prohibition.

7 THE AGE OF
PROHIBITION
(1917–1933)

(*previous page*)
In 1926 Congressman
William Upshaw of
Georgia was determined to
keep the country "dry." He
lost the battle when
Prohibition was repealed in
1933.
(*Library of Congress*)

7

FAILURE OF THE WETS

Perhaps the most surprising fact about the march of the United States from partial Prohibition in 1917 to total Prohibition in 1920 is that the heavy drinkers and especially the regular saloon goers never mounted any organized opposition.

The saloon customers' lives were about to be changed drastically and unpleasantly, but they showed little understanding of the political process and how to influence it. The drys, by way of contrast, were well organized and ceaselessly active on behalf of their cause. Their activities were amply funded, both by the membership and by affluent outside sources. The wets never put together a single major fund-raising effort.

The saloon goers may have been embarrassed by the almost daily revelations, in the newspapers and by preachers, of the saloons' links to prostitution and political corruption.

They were constrained, too, by the outbreak of World War I in 1914, and especially by the entry of the United States into the war in 1917. A veritable torrent of shocking

All bars, saloons, taverns, and other drinking establishments were, of course, closed. So were all breweries and distilleries except those few specifically permitted to produce alcohol for legitimate purposes. Monitoring so many closings was a daunting task. The United States had nearly 178,000 saloons, over 1,200 legal breweries, over 500 legal distilleries, and an uncounted number of illegal installations.

The resulting loss of income was huge. Breweries and distilleries comprised the fifth largest industry in the United States. Their combined annual revenue in the years preceding Prohibition was close to $1 billion.

All liquor stores had to close. Other places of business that sold liquor, such as country stores, had to dispose of their existing stocks and could not replenish them.

The weeks between the enactment of the Volstead Act and its going into effect were marked by a veritable frenzy of liquor-buying as drinkers stocked up.

UNEXPECTED EFFECTS

The drys had optimistically predicted that enactment of national Prohibition would result in a great purification and cleansing of America. Alcoholism would become a thing of the past. No longer would families suffer the neglect or brutality of drunken breadwinners. Nor would they be reduced to poverty by the head of the family's spending his wages on liquor.

These hopes were only partly realized, for ample quantities of illegal liquor soon became available. The working classes and the poor felt the restrictions of Prohibition most directly, for they could ill afford the high prices demanded by the bootleggers.

Cocktails that were priced at fifteen cents in 1918 cost seventy-five cents by the early 1920s. The price of domestic lager beer was $10.50 a barrel in 1918. A mere quart cost from fifteen cents to one dollar more than the original price by 1930. The price per barrel might amount to $160 or more. Again in 1918, a quart of domestic spirits averaged about $1.39. By 1930 the same quantity had gone up to $4.01.

The prices of imported liquors rose even more. A substantial portion of American-made liquor was passed off as imported, drawing the higher prices.

At the start of the Prohibition era, considerably more beer was drunk than spirits. Prohibition changed that. An estimated 75 percent of all pure alcohol drunk during Prohibition was consumed as spirits (i.e., whiskey, gin, brandy, or Scotch), and only 15 percent was beer.

Prohibition brought with it other undesirable effects that were unexpected. The drys had grossly underestimated the drinkers' appetite for liquor, their determination to obtain it, and their willingness to break the unpopular law if necessary.

The first and most significant result was the rapid development of illegal bootleg organizations of a size and scope never seen before. The bootleggers proved enormously efficient at working with local bootleggers, buying up their product, diluting it, and finding customers for it. They also obtained ample supplies of liquor from Europe, Canada, Mexico, Cuba, and the West Indies. They organized networks for distribution and sold the liquor in every corner of the nation. Eager customers were only too glad to buy it at outrageous prices.

Seagram, a Canadian distiller, was a small mail-order

liquor business and local whiskey maker when Prohibition first became American (but not Canadian) law. It rapidly developed into one of the world's largest and most successful businesses during Prohibition. The company simply stepped up production and sold to all buyers for cash, asking no bothersome questions. The buyers came in droves, and the profits were huge.

The Seagram's label came to be accepted as evidence that the liquor inside was "the real stuff," or quality merchandise. Actually, it often wasn't, as the bootleggers customarily adulterated this brand as they did all others. Or the label might be counterfeited, as was done with most well-known brands.

Normally, the United States maintained a three-mile limit on its surrounding waters; that is, all waters within three miles of U.S. territory were considered to be under American jurisdiction. To make things harder for the "rumrunners," as the shippers of illegal liquor were known, the United States extended the limit to twelve miles.

The rumrunners simply kept the big, liquor-carrying freighters outside the twelve-mile line. There they unloaded their cargo onto specially designed, powerful speedboats that could outrun the patrolling Coast Guard cutters. The line of bootleg ships stationed outside the limit soon became known as "Rum Row."

By the time the bootleg liquor reached the average American consumer, much of it had been heavily watered down. In that form the same amount of liquor could be sold more profitably to more customers. And besides, the customers were so eager for the liquor, and so grateful to get it, that they almost always accepted it as it came. Customer complaints were rare.

Much of the bootleg liquor was of domestic rather than foreign origin. Numerous illegal distilleries and breweries were in operation, and the men who ran them found ways to obtain liquor's essential ingredients.

But some of the bootleg product was made under more dubious circumstances and of doubtful raw materials. It often contained poisonous wood alcohol, methyl alcohol, or industrial alcohol rather than drinkable grain alcohol. A substantial though inexactly known number of customers lost their sight or their lives when they drank the contaminated liquor.

Homemade liquor was on the market, too. Much of this "bathtub gin" or "home brew" was concocted from alcohol-based hair oil or, even more unbelievably, from automobile antifreeze. Since it was mostly made in people's private homes, Prohibition agents could not legally search for it and the law was simply unenforceable.

Many Italian immigrants were accustomed to making wine at home for family use. Some of them, responding to the virtually unquenchable public demand for all sorts of wines and liquors, began to produce for profit. Their product, not always made with such meticulous care as the family wines, came to be called "red ink." These wine makers made lots of money, but sometimes had to share their new prosperity with local bootleggers. The mobsters regarded any intruders on the local markets as fair game for extortion or "protection" rackets.

THE MAKING OF "MOONSHINE"

One other source of domestic liquor was the "moonshiners." These rural bootleggers, many of them farmers, had been making and distributing bootleg liquor for years. Moonshine probably got its name from the fact that it was usually bottled and sold under cover of darkness

Long before Prohibition the moonshiners had been producing a good strong whiskey that they could sell for relatively little, since they had paid no state or federal taxes on it.

Many moonshiners expanded their operations during the years of Prohibition, and some became quite wealthy. They could hardly have functioned so successfully without the bribed cooperation of corrupt "revenooers," as they called the federal revenue agents.

One of the areas where distilling moonshine was stubbornly persistent before, during, and after Prohibition was in east Texas. The moonshiners had their typical jerry-rigged but effective stills near running creeks (essential for uninterrupted supplies of water) deep in the piney woods.

They hid the fermenting corn under piles of straw. They cooked the corn mash while standing ankle-deep in snow or wilting in summer heat. The state or federal agents would scour the woods for moonshiners. They'd sneak up as close to the stills as they could get without being detected, hide under leaves, and attack at the most favorable moment, whacking the stills to bits with axes.

Moonshine is sometimes produced under unsanitary conditions, and can be dangerous or even lethal to drink. It can be as high as 55 percent alcohol, and is often called "white lightning" because it is so potent. The men who make it seem untroubled by this danger. Almost all drink it themselves.

Today, moonshine that strong costs thirteen to fifteen dollars a gallon at the still. The price rises as it is passed from moonshiner to bootlegger to customer. During Prohibition, when demand was abnormally high, the price was higher, and profits were huge.

THE MOB MUSCLES IN

The cities were by far the most important centers of bootlegging and illegal drinking. One reason was that many of them (such as Boston, New York, Philadelphia, and Chicago) contained large ethnic minorities. These groups had long traditions of drinking and resented Prohibition's curbs on their customs.

Secondly the great mass of the customers lived in the cities. Here were the warehouses, transport hubs, and sales facilities that were essential for large-scale operations.

In order to run their bootlegging operations on a scale that matched the huge demand, city bootleggers recruited gangs or mobs sometimes numbering hundreds of men. Many were professional killers. They were used mainly to fight rival mobs, while they protected their own mob's markets by force of arms.

The mob chieftains bribed policemen, judges, and public officials at every level of government. These criminal organizations functioned for years with minimal interference from the authorities.

In some of the larger towns and cities, such as Al Capone's Chicago, the gangs were almost constantly at war with one another. Each gang tried to wipe out all rivals so that it could "muscle in" on the enemy's markets. The death toll was tremendous.

But the fortunate mob bosses who survived made millions. They by no means limited their operations to bootlegging. Gambling and prostitution were probably their second- and third-largest income sources, and no criminal could operate within their territory without paying them tribute. Some owned speakeasies, restaurants, and nightclubs.

At times, the gangs arranged "peace treaties," under which each gang was allotted a specified "territory" for its operations. Other gangs then pledged not to invade or otherwise tamper with this allotted territory. But such treaties rarely lasted long.

Some up-and-coming gang leader was sure to covet another's sheltered market, and war soon broke out anew. Such was the bloodstained origin of what is known today as organized crime.

The gangland history of the Prohibition era was also marked by the rise of the Mafia, which eventually came to control almost all of the mobs. The Mafia was originally an illegal Sicilian organization known for the absolute obedience it exacted from its members. Its barbarous code included the practice of ruthlessly murdering its enemies and members of the organization found guilty of betrayal.

Sicilian mafiosi (members of the Mafia) are thought to have brought the organization with them when they immigrated to the United States. Many of the top mobsters of the Prohibition era were mafiosi. The organization still plays a central role in organized crime today, though bootlegging has largely been superseded by other, more profitable enterprises.

The drys did not anticipate the drinkers' ability to find ways to get liquor and continue imbibing it almost whenever they wished, despite the law. The drys had assumed that the drinkers would reluctantly accept the new law and abide by it. Instead Prohibition had hardly become a reality before the drinkers made their connections with bootleggers and went right on drinking.

Even more of a shock to the prohibitionists was the startling increase in the number of women and young people who took up drinking during the age of Prohibition. College students were a particular cause for concern. Drinking had become part of the freewheeling new lifestyle that was popular on many campuses. To many of the new drinkers, it had somehow become chic and fashionable to violate the law, hobnob with gangster-bootleggers, and drink up.

With all this illegal activity going on all over the country, a cynical contempt for the law and law enforcement spread ominously among the populace. Breaking the law became somehow the "smart" thing to do, and a subject for humor. If respect for law is the fabric that holds American society together, that fabric was in genuine danger.

TROUBLE IN THE BUREAU

The agents of the Prohibition Bureau were recruited almost at random. In the early years no particular qualifications were required, there were no entry standards, and the pay was low. The general quality of the agents was poor. Many turned out to be completely inept at enforcing the law. Others made up for their low salaries by accepting bribes from the bootleggers. Some even accumulated sizable small fortunes that way.

There were a few notable exceptions. Most outstanding was the honest and efficient agent team of Izzy and Moe.

One big mistake made by the newly appointed leaders of the bureau right after the enactment of Prohibition was to promise that they would liberate America from the scourge of alcohol within a few years. As the twenties passed into the thirties, liquor was more prevalent than ever. The stubborn realities contrasted stunningly with the prohibitionists' rosy promises and did not increase the American people's respect for the forces of law and order.

One zealous agent of the Prohibition Bureau raided a political banquet in Massachusetts. He had been tipped off that liquor would be served and was trying to do his duty. Unfortunately for him, his supervisor in the Prohibition Bureau was among the invited guests. The overeager agent was fired.

SPEAKEASIES

Another unexpected effect of Prohibition was the appearance and rapid spread of the speakeasies. These were the illegal drinking places that replaced the saloons and taverns closed by the Volstead Act. Admission to these so-called "private clubs" was limited to those instantly recognized by a doorkeeper as "members," or those who claimed to know somebody in the mob.

Some of these clubs charged a fifty-cent admission or membership fee. Some issued highly prized identification cards to regular customers, which assured the lucky owner of instant admission. Others issued keys that opened the doors; these were known as "key clubs." At less exclusive speakeasies it was sufficient to whisper a certain almost magical formula into the doorman's ear: "Joe sent me."

The speakeasy may have gotten its name from the necessity of conversing in subdued tones within its walls. Some speakeasies evolved into fully functioning nightclubs during the twenties, frequently with big-name entertainment. These could hardly have stayed in business without the bribed assent of the authorities.

PROHIBITION'S BENEFICIAL EFFECTS

Prohibition also brought some benefits. Per capita alcohol consumption dipped to about one-third of the previous level. For twelve years after Prohibition was repealed, the nation's drinking level remained below pre-Prohibition consumption.

Prohibition measurably improved the nation's health. Alcoholism became considerably rarer than it had been. There were far fewer cases of cirrhosis of the liver, a frequently fatal disease resulting in most cases from heavy drinking. The incidence of many other alcohol-related diseases diminished significantly.

Prohibition's positive effect on health was naturally accompanied by a corresponding decline in the death rate— or at least that percentage that was due to drinking. In 1907 the death rate from chronic or acute alcoholism peaked at 7.3 deaths for every 100,000 Americans. In 1920, the first year of Prohibition, it dropped to 1.0. The rate climbed gradually, as supplies of liquor increased (some of this liquor was poisonous), to 4.0 per 100,000 in 1927. For some unknown reason the alcoholism death rate then declined to 2.5 in 1932, the last full year of Prohibition.

To beat the high cost of liquor, and to avoid participating in any illegal activity, many Americans resorted to non-alcoholic beverages such as water, coffee, tea, fruit juices, and soft drinks. Temperance pamphlets of the Prohibition era often contained recipes for all sorts of drinks using these "safe" ingredients. The consumption of Coca-Cola tripled between 1919 and 1930.

A researcher studying the effects of Prohibition on city people found that urban wage earners spent $2 billion less on alcohol in the first few years after the enactment of Prohibition than before. By 1929 these savings had fallen by half, but the figure was still impressive.

Social workers found less poverty in the cities and fewer broken homes. A social work study of 1927 titled *Does Prohibition Work?* found that more wages were being put into savings or spent for family needs. Less drunkenness brought into the home from bars and saloons also meant less violence.

The amount of alcohol consumed during Prohibition has been estimated at about 50 percent less than before. As recently as the years between 1906 and 1910, annual per capita consumption had amounted to 2.6 gallons. An estimate prepared at the Rutgers University Center for Alcohol Studies in 1980 showed that Americans drank less than ever during Prohibition, probably about one gallon of pure alcohol annually per capita.

THE TIDE TURNS

By the late 1920s some of the glaring problems that had developed under Prohibition were becoming apparent to the public. Enforcement in particular was a shambles. When Prohibition was first passed, Wayne Wheeler of the Anti-Saloon League had estimated overoptimistically that enforcement would cost no more than about $5 million a year. In 1923 the secretary of the Treasury told Congress that the yearly cost of stamping out drinking would probably amount to $28 million. Some years later an enforcement official suggested it might cost a staggering $300 million annually.

In 1929 President Herbert Hoover appointed a commission to investigate Prohibition enforcement from top to bottom and present suitable suggestions for reform. Former attorney general George Wickersham was its chairman, and it became known as the Wickersham Commission.

Its report was issued ten months later. The report revealed numerous instances of gross incompetence and corruption in the Prohibition Bureau. While it conspicuously avoided endorsing the Volstead Act, it neither suggested that enforcement be tightened nor that the law be liberalized. It satisfied neither the wets nor the drys.

Another problem arose when several big states either refused to enforce Prohibition, or did so in a decidedly lax fashion. Juries in parts of states where wet sentiments prevailed declined to convict even obviously guilty persons. In New York, for example, some 7,000 persons were arrested for Prohibition infractions between 1921 and 1923. Exactly 27 were convicted. Many states were all too willing to leave enforcement entirely up to the federal authorities.

Meanwhile, support for Prohibition and the temperance movement was weakening. The law's stifling restrictions on individual liberties had grown irksome. Famed attorney Clarence Darrow denounced Prohibition as "an outrage and senseless invasion of the personal liberties of millions of intelligent and temperate persons who see nothing dangerous or immoral in the moderate consumption of alcoholic beverages."

The temperance movement had come increasingly under the sway of uncomprising hard-line leaders; moderates were becoming more and more disaffected. As early as 1918 a retired naval officer formed the Association Against the Prohibition Amendment.

In March 1929 the extremists won what proved a hollow

victory. They got Congress to pass, and the president to sign, the Jones Act. It plugged loopholes in the Volstead Act and increased the penalties for violating the Prohibition act from four months or a $10,000 fine to five years *plus* a $10,000 fine. The Jones Act accomplished little more than heightening the developing public resentment against Prohibition.

Drastic change was in the air.

8 ⋮ REPEAL

(1929–PRESENT)

(previous page)
After Congress repealed
the Eighteenth
Amendment in 1933,
Americans quickly read-
apted to social drinking
patterns—as seen in this
Chicago Southside
tavern in 1941.
(Library of Congress)

8

THE CRASH OF '29 AND THE GREAT DEPRESSION

The 1920s were years of unparalleled prosperity for millions of Americans. Greater numbers than ever before invested their spare cash in the stock market. The prices of most stocks and bonds traded on the stock exchange seemed on an endless upward curve. Stockholders basked in their new wealth.

Most people failed to realize that this sudden affluence was actually built on "paper" fortunes. They were rich only as long as their paper (stocks and bonds) continued to be highly valued.

In October 1929 investors experienced the most disastrous collapse of stock prices in U.S. history. Millions of people, including thousands who owned supposedly safe stocks and bonds in blue-chip corporations (America's top companies), suddenly found that their securities were not worth the gilt-edged paper they were printed on.

The stock market crash was swiftly followed by a nationwide economic collapse. Thousands of industrial and commercial establishments, large and small, closed their doors and went out of business. Mass unemployment was the inevitable result. Soon more wage earners than ever in the nation's entire history—totaling one-fourth of the labor force—were out of work.

What followed has been termed the Great Depression. It comprised a full decade of economic stagnation, marked by disastrously low rates of business investment, meager consumer spending, and widespread economic distress.

EFFECT OF THE DEPRESSION ON PROHIBITION

The depression had almost immediate repercussions on Prohibition. Businessmen and industrialists had generally favored the idea of a dry republic, believing that sober citizens would be more productive employees. But now too many of those same citizens were unemployed or underemployed. They were scarcely able to purchase any of the goods that the depressed economy was still able to produce. Prices had to be lowered to levels that were barely profitable.

Many of the nation's leading businessmen now grew disenchanted with Prohibition. They became convinced that its repeal would remedy at least some of the nation's problems. It would mean a new start for what had been one of the nation's largest and most profitable industries. Unemployment would be diminished as thousands returned to work in the breweries, distilleries, saloons, and taverns. The government would benefit from the tremendous increase in tax revenues.

The American Bar Association, the American Legion, and the American Federation of Labor were among the prominent organizations that came out in favor of repeal.

Women flocked to the newly formed Women's Organization for National Prohibition Reform. In less than two years it recruited nearly a million and a half members.

A new instrument for measuring public opinion, the poll, was used to assay public sentiment for repeal. An influential magazine called *The Literary Digest* conducted a poll of five million telephone subscribers in 1930. It showed that a majority in forty-three states favored either changes in the law or its outright repeal.

TRIUMPH OF THE WETS

In the election campaign of 1932 the Democratic presidential candidate, Franklin Delano Roosevelt, was at first cautious about espousing repeal. Only when he was certain of its popularity and of strong backing from the wets did he come out openly for it. The Republicans, with Herbert Hoover running for reelection, vacillated and never did speak out in favor of repeal. Roosevelt's promise to get rid of Prohibition was a factor in his landslide victory.

One of the first acts of the new administration was to submit the Twenty-first Amendment to Congress, repealing the Eighteenth Amendment, which had established Prohibition only thirteen years earlier. Congress passed the repeal amendment in December 1933. The necessary thirty-six states swiftly ratified it.

Utah was the thirty-sixth state to ratify. The instant the good news was flashed to him, President Roosevelt broadcast it to a jubilant nation.

Roosevelt warned against a celebratory drinking binge, and against the return of the saloon, "either in its old form or in some modern guise."

Though there was some angry talk of defiance by die-hard drys, and some raucous celebrating by wets in a few cities, repeal was generally accepted calmly by the nation as a whole. Drys again attempted to get Prohibition adopted as a patriotic act during World War II—remembering that they had succeeded the first time during World War I—but the new effort got nowhere. And when the Anti-Saloon League tried during the war to get a new Prohibition amendment through Congress, it failed as well.

America's values had changed. The country as a whole was simply uninterested in the temperance message. The result was a drastic shrinkage in the temperance organizations' membership. By the mid-1960s the WCTU—once a million and a half strong—could barely muster 250,000 members. The Anti-Saloon League had practically disappeared.

REPEAL IN THE STATES

When repeal was passed, North Dakota, Kansas, and Oklahoma joined five southern states in retaining Prohibition. Enforcement was spotty, at best. Florida blithely contradicted itself, voting for the Twenty-first Amendment but keeping a tough dry law. This law was neither funded nor enforced, however.

Other states enacted various kinds of limitations on the sale of liquor within their borders. They generally were aimed at preventing the reappearance of saloons. In a few states restrictions were placed on the amounts of liquor that wholesalers could sell to retail liquor outlets, or on liquor advertising.

Almost all the states felt that they must act to prevent the return of the pre-Prohibition social evils that too often accompanied drinking. Every state set up an agency to supervise liquor distribution and sales, but their powers varied greatly. Many states established government monopolies on package sales of distilled liquor (package sales are purchases in quantity, such as by the bottle or carton, and do not include purchases by the drink). The sale of liquor by the drink was banned in Utah.

Pennsylvania, Vermont, and Ohio were among the states that permitted beer to be sold by privately owned businesses. Wine was dealt with similarly in some states.

Of the states and localities that remained dry after repeal, few remained dry by the 1950s. In Oklahoma only beer containing 3.2 percent or less alcohol was legal until 1959, when the state went fully wet. Distilled spirits could not be sold in Mississippi until the mid-1960s. On the other hand, forty New Jersey municipalities still banned all liquor sales.

THE TREATMENT OPTION

Some attention had been paid even before Prohibition to the notion that alcoholics needed some kind of individual treatment. The WCTU, for instance, had long focused its main efforts on individual drunks. But the advent of Prohibition temporarily put an end to public discussion of this approach.

Even after repeal the treatment alternative continued to be ignored. During the 1930s the nation was preoccupied with the struggle to end the depression. During the 1940s the nation was preoccupied with World War II, and then the effort to reconvert the economy to peacetime production.

Drunks were routinely consigned to the justice system. The same ones might be arrested over and over, but they received no treatment. Yet the medical damage caused by drinking was well-known by that time.

ALCOHOLICS ANONYMOUS

One glowing exception stood out from the practice of ignoring the need to treat individual alcoholics. This was Alcoholics Anonymous, or AA as it is familiarly called.

AA grew out of the meeting of two alcoholics in Akron, Ohio, in 1935. Both Bill W. and Dr. Bob were seeking some effective way of treating the disease they shared. They had each independently decided that it might help to discuss the problem with another alcoholic. Each believed that alcoholism is a disease. Each felt powerless to end the addiction alone, without outside encouragement and support.

The two friends agreed to help each other to fight off the previously irresistible lure of drink. Their mutual effort was successful, as each of them avoided drinking. The next step was natural: They felt a moral obligation to help other alcoholics in any way possible. The two pioneers proceeded to spread the good news among other alcoholics that they could help one another to stay sober.

Their idea worked. Groups of alcoholics began to come together spontaneously, applying the self-help principle. The two founders called these meetings a fellowship. In 1939 they gave the fellowship a name: Alcoholics Anonymous. Its fame gradually spread around the world. In the early 1990s there were an estimated 89,215 groups meeting in 132 countries with a membership of over 2 million.

Membership in AA is nonsectarian, interracial, open to all, free of charge, and includes both men and women. The only entry requirement is a firm decision to stop drinking.

AA follows a Twelve-Step system. At Step One members start by admitting that they are powerless over alcohol, and that "their lives [have] become unmanageable." They proceed to Steps Two through Eleven, trying to attain a spiritual renewal, confessing their faults and agreeing to "make amends" to all those harmed in any way by their drunkenness. They pledge to trust in God, who alone can enable them to live without drinking.

AA has thus far helped approximately one million alcoholics to reform.

AA does not expect that every member will put his or her faith in the same God. Many interpretations are possible. A member may, for example, choose to believe in the AA chapter as the Higher Power in which to trust.

In Step Twelve the member makes a commitment to "carry this message to all alcoholics, and to practice these principles in all affairs."

At AA meetings members use only their given names, remaining otherwise anonymous. They are welcome to tell their stories to the assembled group, no matter how sad or painful or self-revealing. They are secure in the knowledge that no one will laugh at them or scorn them or criticize them, but that everyone present will respond sympathetically and positively.

At almost all AA meetings the members usually recite the following Serenity Prayer in unison:

> *God grant me the serenity*
> *to accept the things I cannot change;*
> *Courage to change*
> *the things I can, and*
> *Wisdom to know the difference.*

Certain additional needs had become apparent by the 1970s, and the members set up two new groups that functioned in cooperation with AA but were independent from it. These were Al-Anon, focusing on the special problems experienced by alcoholics' families and other loved ones, and Alateen, which seeks to help alcoholics' teenage children.

To avoid controversy, AA does not permit its central body or its local chapters to become embroiled in politics.

Of all forms of treatment available to alcoholics, AA has the best record. A higher percentage of its members stop drinking and then stay sober than any other group.

Sober members are termed "recovering alcoholics." They consider themselves to be afflicted with the disease of alcoholism for the rest of their lives. They can never again take so much as one drink, and they must continue to attend AA meetings.

Various studies have given a variety of reasons for AA's unique record of success. The spiritual rebirth that the members experience as they traverse the Twelve Steps is often cited. The psychological support of the group that members can rely on is another strong reason. So are the AA practices that reshape the recovering alcoholic's entire lifestyle. The AA method has frequently been likened to a restorative form of group therapy.

AA has not been alone in labeling alcoholism as a disease. The American Medical Association and the American Hospital Association passed resolutions in the mid-1950s recommending that treatment be predicated on the disease theory.

TREATMENT FOR THE CHILDREN OF ALCOHOLICS

That the children of alcoholics have special psychological and emotional needs has been recognized increasingly in recent years. They often face an "Elephant-in-the-Living-Room" situation. It is as if there were a huge monster living with the family. The "monster" is actually the fact that one or both parents have a drinking problem and behave erratically because of it. The rest of the family is all too keenly aware of the problem but tries very hard to ignore it.

Children who live with this predicament, suppressing their feelings, often express themselves through troublesome behavior. They need to be taught to understand the nature of their parents' problem, and to talk openly and honestly about it. They need to be helped to cope with it and to change.

Many institutions across the country have developed special programs to treat such children. Typical is the ten-week education and support program started in the mideighties by Mercy Medical Center in Rockville Centre, New York. The children meet once a week with children about their own age who have similar difficulties. They learn to talk freely about what it is like to grow up with an alcoholic parent or parents. They learn, above all, that they are not unique and that the family's troubles are not their fault.

Like Mercy, numerous institutions simultaneously conduct workshops for the parents. They try to deal with the entire family, recognizing that alcoholism in one or both parents is a family disease.

RESEARCH INTO ALCOHOLISM

The success of AA stimulated interest in alcohol-related research. In 1938 a group of scientists who were interested in the subject formed the Research Council on Problems of Alcohol. Its aims were to raise funds for medical research on alcoholism, to prevent alcoholism through public education, to investigate alcohol-related automobile accidents, and in general to study health problems stemming from drinking.

Though the council didn't last very long, it stimulated formation of the Yale Center for Alcohol Studies, which took over most of its functions. Scientific work on alcoholism got under way on a large scale at the center, and a number of important inquiries were eventually carried out.

Since 1962 it has been situated at Rutgers University in New Jersey. In 1948 the center launched what soon became the leading scientific journal in this field. It continues today as the *Journal of Studies on Alcohol*. The center has also been highly influential in popularizing the disease concept of alcoholism.

ALCOHOLISM TREATMENT SPREADS

American businessmen had long been accustomed to firing employees whose work was impaired by alcohol. During the 1940s and 1950s an awareness began to spread among business leaders that this was a needlessly expensive practice. Some of the personnel that companies were losing were highly trained and highly skilled. Many had mastered their jobs and risen in the company, after receiving their training and experience at company expense.

With DuPont taking action as early as 1943, the first to do so, other corporations began to develop programs aimed at rehabilitating employees with alcohol-related problems instead of discharging them. Usually termed employee assistance programs, they have the powerful built-in motivation for the employees of keeping their jobs, and accordingly have high cure rates. They also have enabled their companies to economize substantially by "saving" key personnel instead of training newcomers.

Commercial and industrial enterprises were operating 2,250 such programs in the early 1980s. State governments began to set up a wide variety of programs of their own. The federal government had also shown interest in this field for some time. As early as 1944 the U.S. Public Health Service declared alcoholism America's fourth largest public health problem.

In the 1960s several decisions by the U.S. Supreme Court upheld the disease concept of alcoholism. Congress followed these up in 1970 with the Comprehensive Alcohol Abuse and Alcoholism Prevention Act. This law established a federal agency, the National Institute on Alcohol Abuse and Alcoholism, to focus the government's efforts to deal with the plight of alcoholism.

In a sense, the NIAAA assumed many of the roles of the former temperance movement. It never advocated Prohibition, however. It sought to enlighten the public about the problems of alcohol abuse. It sought to shape public policy relating to the resulting problems. NIAAA was a response to the increasingly urgent demand for the federal government to act upon the alcoholism dilemma.

The National Conference of Commissioners on Uniform State Laws drafted a Uniform Alcoholism and

Intoxication Act in 1971, for study and possible adoption by the states. One of its most important provisions ended the jurisdiction of the criminal justice system over many alcohol-related law violations. In the ensuing decade many states adopted this law or modified versions of it.

SCOPE OF THE PROBLEM

The full extent of America's drinking problem first became clear in 1978. The National Institute on Alcohol Abuse and Alcoholism then estimated that 10 percent of Americans who drank were problem drinkers. These were the nation's alcoholics, physically or psychologically addicted to alcohol.

Another 26 percent were classified as having potential problems with alcohol. Drink was damaging their social lives, their economic functioning, or their health.

These figures meant that close to 10 million Americans fit into one of these two categories. No less than 5.75 million were alcoholics. In total, a startling 7 percent of the American population over the age of eighteen were at risk.

The NIAAA also noted that cirrhosis of the liver, a disease most commonly caused by heavy drinking, was the sixth most frequent cause of death in the United States. If all alcohol-related deaths were added together, they would total approximately 205,000 deaths per year.

But that is not all. The NIAAA surmised that there might be as many as 3.3 million additional problem drinkers in the fourteen to nineteen age group. Although other researchers have questioned the NIAAA's figures, suggesting that the true numbers were either higher or lower, no one doubts the report's ultimate message: Problem drinkers constitute a substantial segment of the American population.

Summing up the annual financial losses directly or indirectly due to problem drinking, the NIAAA estimated that they totaled $43 billion. These losses were spread among health care costs, fire losses, social costs incurred in resolving problems brought on by drinking, violent crime, traffic accidents, and loss in production.

The temperance movement could only take bitter satisfaction from the fact that the report verified its own pessimistic predictions.

NEW LIQUOR TAXES AND
NEW LIQUOR REGULATIONS

No sooner was repeal enacted than many localities, states, and the federal government quickly voted new and quite burdensome taxes on liquor. The federal tax on distilled spirits amounted to fully two dollars per gallon. It was expected to bring in revenues of $400 million.

Certain other "nuisance taxes" that had been in effect under Prohibition were done away with. These included a federal tax of one-half cent on each gallon of gasoline, a 5 percent tax on excess profits, and an equal tax on dividends. They had brought the government only slightly more than half the estimated new liquor revenues.

A new Federal Alcohol Control Administration was established, but it was bound by the law to allow the states maximum leeway in liquor affairs.

It may be worth noting at this point that the federal government has evinced a lively interest in excise taxes on alcoholic beverages over the past half century. In 1944 the tax on distilled spirits was $.50 per proof gallon. As of January 1, 1991 (the latest date for which figures are available), it had multiplied many times and stood at $13.50. The tax on light wines (not over 14 percent alcohol) in 1944 was $.15 per wine gallon. The 1991 tax was $1.07. And the 1944 tax on beer was $8.00 per 31-gallon barrel. In 1991 the figure was more than double, at $18.00.

Exactly how much did these excises bring in to the U.S. government? In 1959 alcohol taxes alone raked in more than $3 billion. The total excise tax revenue that year was not quite $11 billion. By 1990 the total excise intake had soared to almost $39 billion. Alcohol excises made up nearly $6 billion of that.

It is interesting to note that the amounts taken in by the federal government from alcohol taxes in both 1959 and 1990 exceeded the revenues from tobacco, automobiles, other automotive products, and all other commodities subject to excise taxes.

MORE LEGACIES OF PROHIBITION

Strong public sentiment had supported repeal. It clearly indicated that the American people no longer viewed drinking as some kind of immoral, inherently evil, or antisocial behavior. Instead they by and large accepted it as a normal leisure-time activity.

Yet Prohibition did leave some traces of its passage on public conduct. After repeal a surprising number of individuals who might once have been drinkers never resumed their former habit. It is not clear whether they were motivated to become teetotalers by being converted to temperance or to religion, or were reformed by some other influence. Some of them might have grown up during Prohibition, and might never have started drinking at all.

An estimated 30 percent of all Americans over the age of eighteen abstained from drinking after repeal. About the same proportion were staying away from alcoholic beverages fifty years later, in the 1980s.

Despite the gloomy warnings of the prohibitionists, repeal was not the signal for a sudden and dramatic increase in alcohol consumption. In 1934, the first year after repeal, Americans drank one gallon of alcohol per capita. Consumption did not rise to the pre-Prohibition level of two gallons per capita until about 1945.

Still, drinkers (defined as persons who drank any amount of liquor at any time) were the majority. Their alcohol consumption did go up to a peak of 2.8 gallons per person by the late 1970s. After that, according to a 1978 report by the National Institute on Alcohol Abuse and Alcoholism, consumption leveled off. NIAAA was unable to suggest a reason.

The same NIAAA report ranked the United States fifteenth in the world in alcohol consumption. The United States was well behind Portugal's 6.27 gallons per year for drinkers over fifteen years old, but roughly comparable to West Germany's 3.75 and Canada's 2.84. Americans drank more than the Irish (2.47) and Swedish (1.84), and considerably more than Israelis (.86).

Americans tended to drink more distilled spirits after repeal, and less beer. Although beer was still the most popular alcoholic beverage in 1934 and has remained so, distilled spirits and wine were catching up. The United States ranked third worldwide in hard liquor consumption, but only thirteenth in beer drinking and a lowly seventeenth in the wine-drinking category.

EDUCATIONAL UNCERTAINTIES

During Prohibition the drys had succeeded in getting "scientific temperance instruction" incorporated into the curricula of most schools. But with Prohibition repealed, the subject seemed much less relevant. By 1935 most school districts had simply eliminated it from the course of study.

Teaching about the "evil" and "enslaving" effects of alcohol was largely restricted to schools in districts that remained dry. Today, with the renewed emphasis on the war against drugs and alcohol, health education courses in schools throughout the country include lessons designed to give students the latest information about the dangers of alcohol, and to discourage alcohol abuse.

The effects of repeal during the first decades after its enactment were mixed. The American people seemed to be in search of some sort of consensus about drinking, but the nation proved too diverse for any single approach to dominate.

9 DRINKING IN THE U.S. TODAY

(previous page)
Each year thousands of
American college students
flock to beaches during
their spring term breaks for
parties, suntanning, and
drinking.
*(B. Daemmrich,
Image Works)*

9

FITNESS AND DRINKING

America's new health and fitness consciousness is one of the most influential factors shaping today's attitudes toward drinking.

"You just can't exercise with a hangover," a thirty-five-year-old woman told an interviewer. "I found I couldn't get through a tough aerobics class after drinking a bottle of wine the night before. . . . I want to go into later life with organs that aren't aged prematurely."

At dinner parties the trend is toward "drinking less but drinking better." Guests prefer expensive wines or imported beers, but drink fewer glasses of them. People seem to be following the advice of famed old-time football coach Knute Rockne: "Drink the first. Sip the second slowly. Skip the third."

Alcoholic drinks are also known to be high in calories. A recent Swiss study showed that the body converts alcohol into fat more readily than any other food.

TODAY'S DEVELOPING NEW ATTITUDES

American society has become increasingly intolerant of alcohol's supposed role in easing social contacts or reducing stress. The vast increase in media attention to the harmful effects of drinking helped to produce this new attitude.

A 1989 Gallup Poll reported that 44 percent of Americans said they were not drinking at all. This level of abstinence was last attained in 1958.

"A big change is going on, and it's going on across the culture," observed Robin Room, a sociologist with the Alcohol Research Group in Berkeley, California. "It's pretty widespread. It's not just happening in one group."

Some experts attribute the decline mainly to the aging of the baby boomers, who no longer make up a large part of the harder-drinking younger age groups. But another Alcohol Research Group analyst argued that the aging of the population accounted for only a fraction of the decline. Changes in attitudes and behavior were more responsible, he said.

Stubbornly unaffected by the decline are the nation's hard-core excessive drinkers. According to 1994 estimates, alcoholics and alcohol abusers in the United States still number about 18 million.

Some of the changed attitudes are most apparent in social situations, formerly centered around drinking. The hilarious drunk might have been the life of the party back in 1980. Today, he is more likely to be treated as an unwelcome pest.

The "three-martini lunch," long popular with businessmen, may be disappearing as employers increasingly question their employees' drinking on the job. Employees themselves recognize the riskiness of being "out of it," or too impaired to do one's job, for part or most of the afternoon.

Meanwhile, liquor companies faced a thirty-year low in sales in the early 1990s. They scrambled to keep profits up. One strategy was to emphasize a company's finer, higher-priced brands. Another, as we shall see, was to develop new markets and to target advertising at specific audiences.

Still another was described by Anita Rosepka, managing editor of Beverage Network, a group of publications. "We are going to see fewer liquor stores," she said, "and those that survive will sell a greater variety of products, including bottled water, food, and party items."

There are some contrary indications, however. Despite the drop in sales reported by most liquor dealers, neighborhood bars with regular customers are doing business about as usual. People still seem to enjoy getting together for relaxed socializing and a few drinks in a friendly setting.

THE CHANGING COLLEGE SCENE

Even many colleges, once bastions of reckless drinking, today see more moderation. It is not unusual to see editorials in college newspapers denouncing on-campus drinking binges, and advocating temperance. These efforts are promoted by student groups such as BACCHUS (Boost Alcohol Consciousness Concerning the Health of University Students) and SADD (Students Against Drunk Driving). Working off-campus but highly effective is MADD (Mothers Against Drunk Driving).

Spring break used to be a time when college students gathered on beaches like Daytona Beach in Florida for wild drinking sprees and seemingly endless parties. These were characterized by monumental chugalug contests that often left the competitors violently sick to their stomachs, unconscious, or worse.

Students used to proudly sport T-shirts reading PARTY TILL YOU PUKE. Nowadays these have been replaced by posters cautioning students to PARTY SMART. Daytona Beach's hotels and nightclubs now require wristbands or hand stamps certifying that the bearer is of legal age to drink.

One noteworthy difference in today's spring break goings-on is a drop in the number of students killed or injured in falls from condo or hotel balconies.

THE YOUNG AGAINST DRUNK DRIVING— BUT STILL GETTING DRUNK

At the same time, nationwide drives against alcohol abuse by the young have resulted in significant gains. Traffic deaths due to drunk driving involving youngsters from sixteen to nineteen declined by 39.1 percent from 1982 to 1990. They remained the number one killer of young people aged sixteen to twenty-four, however.

The Office of Substance Abuse Prevention (OSAP) in the U.S. Department of Health and Human Services has launched a Put on the Brakes campaign that has publicized the harm that alcohol does to youth.

OSAP spokesman Lewis D. Eigen voiced his agency's concern: "We're getting reports from all over that kids are not just getting drunk inadvertently at a party, but as a result of intentionally downing the greater and greater amounts of alcohol that are needed to get that effect."

PREVENTION

Reginald Smart, director of prevention studies at the Toronto Addiction Foundation, believes there may be a natural limit to any country's alcohol consumption. "When consumption hits a certain level, it tends to level off. Once you get too many social problems and too high a death rate, then countries begin to take steps." Taxes, regulations, and other government controls are among these steps. Temperance movements have used them throughout history.

A subject that has come to the fore in recent years is the prevention of drunkenness without resorting to Prohibition. One frequently mentioned means of accomplishing this is by reducing and then controlling the availability of liquor to the public.

Several states have already taken steps in this direction. They have passed laws that require liquor to be purchased in packaged-goods stores, which are usually but not always state-owned. The liquor must then be drunk off-premises (that is, somewhere away from the store).

Evidence drawn from other countries and from America's own Prohibition experience shows that making liquor less convenient to purchase reduces the amount of liquor consumption, and also cuts down on drinking-related problems.

But limiting access to liquor might not be enough. Other steps would have to be taken, all openly aimed at discouraging drinking. They would probably have to include education about alcohol and its effects, strict control of liquor advertising, taxes on alcoholic beverages to keep their prices high, and rigorous regulation of liquor sales.

An important step has already been taken by the states, with powerful encouragement from the federal government. They have all voted to raise the minimum drinking age to twenty-one. It had been lowered to eighteen in many places in the 1970s.

The question of a proper minimum age for purchasing liquor was hotly debated. Impressive evidence was adduced to show that raising the age would significantly reduce traffic accidents. Counter evidence, often just as impressive, challenged this conclusion.

Federal action finally tipped the balance in 1984. A law was passed cutting federal highway moneys to any states where the allowable drinking age was under twenty-one. States that had not yet raised the minimum legal age hastened to do so.

Adults have generally supported raising the legal drinking age. Understandably, the eighteen to twenty age group has emphatically opposed it.

THE DIVIDED AMERICAN MIND

Despite all this activity centered on alcohol's uses and abuses, Americans still harbor often contradictory notions about drinking. An incident from the 1970s illustrates this. During that decade the National Institute on Alcohol and Alcoholism launched an ad campaign around the theme Drink Responsibly. Other groups joined in, including some voices from the alcoholic-beverage industry.

Dissent began to be heard from various sources, particularly those groups that were trying to discourage drinking. They argued that "responsible drinking" frequently led to problem drinking. NIAAA should never endorse drinking, responsible or not. Embarrassed, NIAAA withdrew the campaign—only to anger those who had approved it and published advertisements on the same theme.

NIAAA has come under fire for other reasons. Studies conducted by impartial scholars have accused the institute of inflating its statistics on the number of alcoholics and on the effects of drinking on the economy. NIAAA allegedly exaggerated these figures in order to enhance its own importance and to justify its expenses.

What kinds of drinking behavior are allowable? NIAAA has pointed to the need for "a new national consensus concerning what constitutes responsible use and nonuse of alcoholic beverages." This is certainly a laudable aim. The trouble is that the American people have not yet arrived at any such agreement. As a result, no clear national policy on alcohol consumption is possible.

Yet there are certain subjects in this field on which nationwide agreement does exist. Americans seem to have decided once and for all, for example, that national Prohibition is a thing of the past. They have not made public statements to that effect; nevertheless the overwhelming majority have agreed that drinking shall henceforward be legal in the United States.

One other unspoken agreement exists. Having chosen to be a drinking nation, Americans seem prepared to tolerate the problems that inevitably follow. They accept just two kinds of restrictions on the right to drink. One is insisting on a legal drinking age of twenty-one. The other concerns driving, and demands severe punishments for driving under the influence.

Both stem from the public's well-justified alarm about the staggering toll of drinking-related automobile accidents.

Drinking is a factor in no fewer than one of every two fatal accidents. Traffic accidents are the leading cause of death for people between the ages of five and thirty-four. Nearly one-third of all alcohol-related traffic deaths are caused by problem drinkers or alcoholics.

In the relatively short period from 1982 through 1986, approximately 100,000 people died in alcohol-related crashes. This amounts to an average of one such death every twenty-two minutes.

Of all alcohol-related deaths, 27 percent were due to motor vehicle accidents. Homicides, suicides, and non-motor vehicle accidents accounted for 34 percent. The remaining 39 percent were caused by cirrhosis of the liver and other medical consequences of heavy drinking.

Cirrhosis is the principal factor in chronic liver disease. A largely preventable illness, liver disease is nevertheless the nation's ninth leading cause of death. In recent years, as Americans have drunk less, the death rate resulting from liver disease has declined correspondingly. From 1980 through 1989 this particular rate of mortality dropped 23 percent, the Centers for Disease Control and Prevention reported.

During these same years, according to the National Institute on Alcohol Abuse and Alcoholism, drinking declined to its lowest rate since 1968. This decline was one of the main reasons for a parallel drop in deaths from motor vehicle accidents in 1992. Not only were fewer people drinking; fewer were drinking and driving.

The death rate from liver disease in men was more than twice as high as for women, 14.7 percent per 100,000 versus only 6.6 percent. The rate for blacks was higher than for whites. Explanations for these differences are not yet available.

In 1986 the secretary of health and human resources proposed to Congress a new national plan to combat alcohol abuse and alcoholism. It estimated the financial costs to the nation of alcohol-related health care problems, loss of productivity, work lost by the victims of alcohol-related accidents and crimes, and the incarceration of criminals.

The report also projected these estimated costs into the future. In 1983 dollars the costs for that year were $116.9 billion. In 1990 they rose to $136.3 billion. By 1995 they would add up to $150 billion.

But these projections will be accurate only if the nation's drinking patterns remain constant. Actually, the nation has been gradually cutting down on its drinking since about 1980.

THE EXPANDING WAR ON ALCOHOLISM

Across the nation the war against alcoholism has grown into a veritable industry. Its workers are physicians, psychiatrists, psychologists, social workers, nurses, and licensed counselors. In addition, large numbers of volunteers, mostly employed by organizations of various kinds, attempt to deal with the nation's estimated 18 million problem drinkers, almost twice the number in 1978.

To cope with so vast a problem, the lists of alcoholism fighters are still growing. In New York State, for example, the number of state-licensed treatment facilities has virtually doubled within the last few years, rising from 269 in 1983 to 485 in 1990. And yet, according to Richard Chady, spokesman for the State Office of Alcoholism and Substance Abuse Services, "We're still treating only about 10 percent of the people in need every year."

An approximate count was recently done of the makeup of the treatment population. Males outnumbered females by more than three to one: about 217,000 to about 63,000. Classifying the patients racially, the more than 200,000 whites were the most numerous group. African Americans ranked second, with over 44,000. Then came Latinos, with almost 27,000; and then Native Americans, with close to 11,000. Asian Americans had by far the lowest number in treatment: an infinitesimal 900 or so.

These figures must be treated with caution, however. Roughly 60 percent of alcoholics probably go undiagnosed.

ALTERNATIVES TO ALCOHOLICS ANONYMOUS

AA defines alcoholism as a disease, yet never prescribes or endorses any drug or medication. It operates no medical or inpatient facilities. The AA chapters do not schedule any outside doctors as guest speakers.

AA does have a pronounced tilt toward spirituality or religion. Having admitted their powerlessness over alcohol, the members pledge to put themselves entirely and trustingly in the hands of God or some vague Higher Power, referred to repeatedly in AA's famous Twelve-Step program. Nowhere in the program is any specific religion or denomination mentioned.

About 50,325 chapters of AA now operate throughout the U.S. They have about 1.1 million members. Some chapters meet as often as fifteen times a week. They meet in houses of worship, hospitals, prisons, public libraries, and many other types of institutions.

Although there were no AA chapters for young people before 1970, such chapters now exist all over the United States. Some have sizable teen memberships.

Many potential members of AA are alienated by its religious orientation. They prefer a secular and rational approach, with due credit allowed to every individual who attains sobriety. At the same time, they carefully avoid any direct criticism of AA or its unrivaled record of success.

Two of the national groups that offer alternatives to AA's spiritual emphasis are Secular Organizations for Society, also known as Save Our Souls (SOS), and Rational Recovery.

Founded in 1986, SOS is headquartered in North Hollywood, California. There are SOS affiliates for the families and friends of alcoholics. Rational Recovery is headquartered in Lotus, California. Private clinics and outpatient treatment centers are everywhere to be found, many with physicians and psychologists on their staffs.

MATCHING TREATMENTS TO PATIENTS

One of the greatest difficulties lies in choosing the modes of treatment that are really effective. There is no certainty about what may work for any particular alcoholic and what may not.

"We've been very successful in reducing the stigma," said Paul Wood, chairman of the National Council on Alcoholism and Drug Dependence. He added that the number of people applying for treatment has also gone up. "There are various successful treatments. But where we've been less successful is in matching the most effective treatment to an individual's specific need."

Dr. Joseph Kern, director of alcoholism treatment services in Nassau County, New York, declared that alcoholism was "the largest public health problem in the country, bar none. . . . Every time we open a new service, in a short time it's filled."

CO-DEPENDENTS

It has been estimated that for each alcoholic, five or six other people are affected. They may include family members, friends, co-workers, employers, and such governmental agencies as the police, courts, and social services. Exact figures are not available, but it is estimated that at least two-thirds of the population is either addicted or affected.

There are many ways in which those closely related to problem drinkers may unwittingly encourage them to continue drinking. The drinker's habit may be a constant subject of discussion, so that the drinker gets the gratifying impression that he or she is the center of everyone's attention. Family members may constantly squabble, so that drinkers' homes are often so filled with tension that the drinkers wish only to escape into the benumbed state of drunkenness.

Or the families may try to "protect" drinkers by making excuses for them and getting them out of embarrassing drunken scrapes. They might, for example, pay off the drinker's debts and then extract the drinker's promise to stop, which all too often proves worthless.

These patterns are termed "co-dependency," in which others, with only the best intentions, actually nurture the drinker's habit.

In unhappy homes family members often tend to seek relief through some sort of substance abuse. The addiction then passes from one generation to another. Unhappy children often grow into unhappy adults. Their offspring are highly likely to be psychologically damaged, as their parents were.

Drinking is also harmful to the stability of marriages. Those in which one or both spouses drink are seven times more likely than nondrinking marriages to end in separation or divorce.

All addictions, whether drug or alcohol, have the same characteristics. The addict feels an irresistible compulsion and accompanying loss of control, resorts to a chemical substance for mental and emotional relief, uses it, and then abuses it regardless of its adverse consequences.

At the beginning the substance abuse gives pleasure, relief from stress, relaxation. The addict believes himself or herself to be in control and able to stop at any time. Eventually the habit becomes stressful, and goes completely out of control. The addict develops a tolerance for the drug or drink. More of it is needed each time to achieve the desired effect.

One in every four American families has at least one alcoholic member or some type of drinking problem. Some 88 million people are either addicted or related to an alcoholic. The United States is home to thirty million children of alcoholics.

TREATMENT DILEMMAS

In the past, doctors were actively discouraged from trying to help alcoholics. No type of treatment seemed reliable. Trying to treat alcoholics was regarded as a waste of time.

Today, treatment centers are located throughout the country. They employ a wide variety of techniques. Many kinds of treatment programs incorporate elements of AA's Twelve-Step method or simply insist that patients attend AA meetings as part of their treatment.

An especially complex problem is the treatment of

women alcoholics. Although they are fewer than men, their numbers are catching up fast. According to the National Council on Alcoholism and Drug Dependence, women in AA chapters already make up 35 percent of the membership. Counselors who work with women point to a whole range of problems affecting women that society needs to deal with.

For instance: What restrictions, if any, need to be placed on the marketing of alcoholic beverages specifically targeted at women? Should health warnings have been placed on liquor bottles earlier, so that women drinkers (men, too, benefited from this protection) could become informed consumers (signs posted in many drinking establishments already warn pregnant women of the effects of alcohol on the unborn)? How do the laws relating to child custody, abuse, and neglect impact on the woman drinker? Are the highway safety laws in any way biased against women who drink?

DRINKING IN THE MOVIES AND ON TELEVISION

In old silent films and in talkies until about 1945, drinking and drunkenness were usually treated as subjects for comedy. Three other customary contexts for drinking were often depicted. One occurred when a group or an individual was about to take some perilous risk and needed to build up their courage. The second occurred to soften the shock of bad news or sorrow. Lastly, drinking usually accompanied scenes of celebration.

Most recent films and TV shows have taken a different approach. Apparently aware that there is nothing inherently funny about people suffering from a debilitating illness, the movies and TV portray alcoholism—on those rare occasions when they portray it all—as a serious problem.

But this is not even remotely true of the movies' and TV's portrayal of drinking scenes. Media characters drink far more, and about six times more frequently, than real-life people. Yet they rarely suffer blackouts, hangovers, sexual dysfunction, or fatal car crashes.

During every hour of prime-time TV, four or five drinking episodes are shown. Children see three thousand such episodes every year. By the time they are eighteen, they will have seen 100,000 beer commercials.

A recent issue of *Adolescent Counselor* magazine reported that eight- to twelve-year-old boys were able to name more brands of alcoholic beverages than U.S. presidents. The Center for Science in the Public Interest polled one hundred students. "One young girl correctly wrote the names of fourteen alcoholic beverages, but could only name four presidents," the center reported. One boy spelled brand names correctly, "but gave presidents' names as 'Nickson' and 'Rosselvet.' " A 1987 survey by *Weekly Reader* found that only 50 percent of fourth graders knew that whiskey, wine, and beer contained a drug.

Only a few movies or TV shows have attempted to present serious depictions of alcoholism. The first was 1945's Academy Award-winning *The Lost Weekend*. It was a harrowing portrayal of an alcoholic on a drinking binge that eventually landed him in a hospital ward for drunken derelicts. This film has been criticized by some alcoholics and counselors on the sole ground that its central character didn't join AA by the film's end.

A later film about a married couple who both became alcoholics was adapted from a TV show, the form in which it was originally shown. It was called *The Days of Wine and Roses*. In this story the husband did eventually join AA and quit drinking, but the wife was unable and unwilling to follow his example.

DRINKING AND CRIME

Back in 1983 a survey was taken that indicated the extent of alcohol use among convicted offenders, just before they committed the crime for which they were currently serving time in prison. The greatest percentage by far, 54 percent, were alcohol users who had committed violent crimes. Only 40 percent were convicted of crimes against property. A third category, often overlapping the other two, includes criminals guilty of drug-related crimes. It is true that fully 69 percent had committed crimes that violated public order, but most of the crimes in this category were minor.

In homicide cases at least one-half of the killers were under the influence. Alcohol was a factor in one-quarter of all suicides.

10 THOSE GLAMOROUS LIQUOR ADS

(previous page)
In 1991 liquor billboards
in New York City were
whitewashed by protesters
accusing the advertisers
of targeting minority
communities as
"untapped markets."
(Jim Wilson, NYT Pictures)

10

THE INDUSTRY'S ADVERTISING CODES

The United States is a drinking nation, but it would be inaccurate to call it a nation of drunkards. Most drinkers drink moderately, and are able to exercise reasonable self-control most of the time.

Those who advertise, market, and promote liquor are understandably eager to increase sales. They are supposedly kept in check by the high-sounding advertising codes that all branches of the industry have voluntarily adopted. The codes serve many purposes, but the principal one is to show the government that the industry is capable of regulating itself. Only a minimum of government regulation is therefore necessary, says the industry.

The advertising codes imply a pledge by the industry to the public.

THE THREE "LIQUOR INDUSTRIES"

The term *liquor industry* has been used so far in this book to include the manufacturers of all alcoholic beverages.

For reasons of precision and clarity, it will be used from this point forward in a more strictly limited sense.

Liquor industry actually encompasses three separate but related industries. First is the distilled spirits industry, which manufactures whiskey, brandy, rum, and other products through a process of distillation. Second is the wine industry, which produces its products from wine grapes by a process of fermentation. The third and largest of all is the beer industry, which makes its products by brewing them.

THE INDUSTRY'S ETHICAL ADVERTISING CODES

The three liquor industries have voluntarily created ethical advertising codes that prohibit or restrict certain kinds of advertising. No print ads, no TV or radio commercials are permitted that target vulnerable groups within the population, such as children, young people, women, and heavy drinkers. Up to the early 1980s the distillers voluntarily agreed that hard liquor should not be advertised on the air. About 1982 this particular self-restriction began to break down.

At no time did the ban on hard liquor ads on radio and TV apply to wines or beer. The codes written by the trade association of the wine industry, the Wine Institute, and the Beer Institute, were more rigorous in some ways than the distillers' code.

Wine ads that urged immoderate drinking were forbidden. So were ads that encouraged wine drinking while engaging in any dangerous activity or while driving. Whereas it was common for liquor or beer ads to picture well-dressed and relaxed people enjoying stylish or affluent lifestyles, the wine code flatly states: "Any attempt to suggest that wine contributes to success or achievement is unacceptable." It adds: "Wine shall not be presented as being essential to personal performance, social attainment, achievement, success or wealth."

All three codes (liquor, wine, and beer) prohibit ads or commercials that seek to enlarge the market for alcoholic beverages. They must not try to persuade nondrinkers to drink or drinkers to drink more. No lewd, false, or sexually provocative material may appear in any liquor ad or commercial. The trouble is that the published ads frequently violate the code rules, both in letter and spirit.

The codes do not mention marketing, merchandising, or promotional materials and activities. The most familiar of these materials are probably the liquor industry's colorful and attractive posters. But the category covers a wide range of other industry-sponsored activities. The ethics underlying some of these seem questionable in that they often seek to accomplish the goals explicitly forbidden by the codes.

Rock concerts, sports events, and broadcasts of sports events are among the industry's favorite sponsored activities. The audiences, obviously, are made up mostly of young people. But according to the industry's own codes, the young constitute a supposedly forbidden target.

The most blatant violators are domestic distributors that are not members of the liquor industry trade associations, foreign wine makers, and certain producers of rum and tequila. Code violations, whether by domestic or foreign companies, have one overriding reason: The companies quite naturally wish to enlarge their market and increase sales. All business enterprises seek to do this.

But the products the liquor companies offer for sale are

unlike other businesses' merchandise (except the tobacco industry); the liquor industry sells products that contain a powerful drug (alcohol).

That is why the federal government insists on having a hand in the regulation of alcohol advertising. Two agencies share this responsibility. One is the Federal Trade Commission, which checks on all advertising; the other is the Treasury Department's Bureau of Alcohol, Tobacco, and Firearms.

EXPANDING THE MARKET

An example of the reasoning behind code violations is a campaign undertaken by the leading beer brewer, Anheuser-Busch, in the 1980s. The company president, Dennis Long, spoke candidly of his "great confidence that there is still considerable room for us to grow." Soon afterward, the company announced new capital expenditures to be used for augmenting the capacity of its breweries by 27 percent within five years.

Obviously, the company intended to market more beer to more beer drinkers. It totally ignored the brewers' code prohibition against efforts to enlarge the market.

Wine makers are equally susceptible to the temptation of going after more customers. An industry analyst and consultant recently expressed his conviction that the wine industry had the possibility of expanding its "user base" by no less than 75 percent. Moreover, he said, persons who were already wine drinkers could be persuaded to drink more. All that was needed was for light drinkers to be "nudged up" to medium, and medium drinkers to heavy.

Light drinkers are usually defined as those who consume

0.1 to 0.21 ounces of alcohol a day. Moderate drinkers consume on the average 0.22 to 0.99 ounces, and heavy drinkers average about 1.0 or more ounces (about two drinks). Heavy drinkers have been estimated as forming up to 20 percent of all adults. They drink most of the hard liquor, wine, and beer that is sold.

A widely shared opinion in liquor industry circles holds that advertising by any brand benefits all brands of the same category. In this view any liquor advertisement is more like a shotgun than a rifle. It hits many targets simultaneously, from light drinkers to medium to heavy, even including non-drinkers, and thus sells its advertised product to more customers.

At the same time that the industry cannot resist reaching out to potential new customers, and trying to persuade drinkers to drink more, it does a certain amount of public-service advertising. Many of these ads urge moderation in drinking.

One of the government's earliest attempts to limit liquor advertising's effect on youth occurred during the Bush Administration (1989–1993). In the summer of 1991, Antonia Novello, then surgeon general, met with executives from the liquor, beer, and wine companies. A joint statement was issued afterward, urging government-industry cooperation and pledging renewed efforts against underage drinking.

Though liquor sales were on the decline in the early 1990s, the liquor companies responded to Novello's alarm by publishing more of these public-service ads than ever. The ad campaign used such slogans as Think Before You Drink and Drink Responsibly. An avowed goal was to remind young people that they had to be at least twenty-one to drink.

Critics of industry public-service ads say these are only a false front put on by the big brewers. Their real purpose is said to be to fend off any new legislation that might put new restrictions on their estimated $2 billion annual advertising and marketing efforts.

The beer companies' slogans have been called "vague" and "meaningless." "Every college kid who is throwing up on his shoes at 1 A.M. thinks that he has been drinking responsibly," said one Wellesley College professor.

But a professor of applied health at Indiana University maintained: "Heavy drinking among students has been a tradition for a thousand years. It's always been a part of student life."

The alcohol industry denies that it targets youth. "You do not target your resources at audiences that cannot buy your products," said a Beer Institute spokesman. He made no mention of the obvious fact that underage youngsters, whose ideas about drinking are all too often shaped by liquor ads, soon mature into drink-buying adults.

Another recent survey, taken by the National Association of Student Councils, produced the same result. Three-fourths of Americans believe the teen drinking problem has worsened in recent years, a 1990 poll revealed.

In November 1991 the surgeon general issued a new blast at the liquor industry's advertising policies, saying that the ads send a "mixed message" to the nation's youth. She singled out TV commercials for wine and beer that show bikini-clad women and athletic men playing sports: "The ads [would] have youth believing that instead of getting up early, exercising, going to school, and playing a sport, all they have to do to fit in is to drink the right alcoholic beverage."

She pointed out that the liquor companies may publicly condemn teen drinking, but they are clearly targeting young people in their ads. The outstanding example was a TV spot for St. Ides malt liquor. It featured the rap star Ice Cube chanting, "In a black can, why don't ya grab a six-pack and get your girl in the mood quicker . . . with St. Ides malt liquor."

It is not hard to understand why alcohol ads use sexy models. In November 1991 Boston University marketing Professor John E. Calfee offered an explanation to the House Select Committee on Children, Youth, and Families: "Faced with . . . the necessity of gaining consumer attention amid overwhelming media clutter, alcohol advertising uses the same techniques that are used in other mature markets, such as automobiles, cosmetics, soap, clothing."

Industry spokesmen point out that the Federal Trade Commission and Secretary of Health and Human Services Louis Sullivan under President Bush rejected the idea of a possible influence of advertising on alcohol consumption. They cite a 1990 Roper Poll that queried young people as to where they got their ideas about various things, including alcoholic beverages. Schoolmates and friends were named by 70 percent, parents by 48 percent, seeing people drink by 12 percent, and advertising by only 8 percent.

More recently, the NBC "Nightly News" program ran a feature on teen alcohol abuse. Afterward, Fred Meister, president of the Distilled Spirits Council of the United States (DISCUS) wrote a letter to anchorman Tom Brokaw. He said that NBC had neglected to mention the recent decline in underage drinking. The feature had also exaggerated the current crackdown on alcohol, in comparison to the campaign against drugs.

A spokesman said the Department of Health and Human Services "has a goal of reducing America's alcohol intake by 20 percent by the year 2000, which is not a goal of the alcoholic beverage industry."

Office of Substance Abuse Prevention spokesman Eigen added, "I don't think it's hysterical to worry about 8,000 to 10,000 kids dying a year from alcohol. . . . If we could wave a magic wand and reduce teen drinkers by a third tomorrow, it would still mean we have a tremendous health problem."

The industry does sponsor public-service ads, many of which attempt to address the public health problem. These ads almost always make the grimmest, most dire predictions. Sample themes include:

- If you think you have a drinking problem, you do.
- A drinking problem can only get worse.
- A drinking alcoholic winds up either dead or institutionalized.
- An individual's efforts to stop drinking on his own are doomed to failure.

An advertising executive for a major treatment center explained the tendency to run the most sensationalist and frightening public-service ads: "We have to run these kinds of ads to keep our market share up. The marketplace is so competitive that it takes nearly constant advertising of this type to keep our telephones ringing."

Yet, if the 105 million drinkers of legal age were to follow the advice of the alcohol counselors and limit their drinking to moderate amounts, liquor, wine, and beer sales would diminish by an estimated 40 percent!

The Target Groups

In trying to expand the market, the liquor industry targets specific groups: light drinkers, heavy drinkers, the young, blacks and other minorities, women, and even people who dislike the taste of alcoholic drinks. The industry develops new kinds of drinks suited to the target groups, and tries to make liquor more convenient to purchase by getting fast-food restaurants, convenience stores, and supermarkets to sell it.

Light drinkers have lately attracted special interest in industry circles. New kinds of beer and wine, called light and containing fewer calories, were put on sale in the 1980s. Today, they make up approximately 15 percent of the total beer market and are selling more every year.

From the brewers' and vintners' points of view, the main purpose of these light beverages is to expand the market, not to encourage drinkers to slim down.

Ads intended for heavy drinkers are designed almost exclusively for males. They often feature "he-men," such as well-known football players. A popular TV campaign by Miller Lite beer, for example, showed athletes jokingly debating the beer's "great taste" versus its "less filling" properties.

But the heavy-drinker category includes large numbers of problem drinkers. Ads aimed at this audience are urging people who are already alcoholics to drink even more. This is a violation of law as well as a departure from industry codes.

The Consumer Protection Division of the Federal Trade Commission looks for these features in judging any ad as violating the law:

- It encourages drinking that amounts to alcohol abuse, such as too much drinking or drinking too fast.
- It plays upon certain known weaknesses of people who are already alcohol abusers to switch brands.
- It tries to dissuade alcohol abusers from cutting down on their consumption.

There is no great mystery as to why the liquor companies try so eagerly to reach the young. The biggest consumers of alcohol are between the minimum drinking age and thirty-four. The greatest percentage of beer drinkers are between eighteen and twenty-four.

Budweiser beer runs ads in college newspapers featuring an "Athlete of the Week." These are otherwise typical Bud ads that show a photo of some local athletic star and a story about an outstanding feat he or she recently performed.

Advertising targeted at young people often seeks to create new drinkers, or to persuade young drinkers to switch brands. The industry considers those in the eighteen to twenty-five category as drinkers, whether they drink or not, because of their age and potential to become drinkers.

According to one beer marketing executive, "Let's not forget that getting a [seventeen- or eighteen-year-old] freshman to choose a certain brand of beer may mean that he will maintain his brand loyalty for the next twenty to thirty-five years. If he turns out to be a big drinker, the beer company has bought itself an annuity."

Young people, including teens and children, are known to be more vulnerable to advertising than adults. Still struggling to win social acceptance, they are eager to learn from the ads' social-role-defining content. That is one reason why sports promotions are so effective.

THE CASE OF THAT SEXY MILLER INSERT

By the spring of 1989 most beer companies were trying to appease the critics of their advertising by increasing the number of their ads emphasizing safety and moderation.

The Miller Brewing Company remained defiant. It produced a sixteen-page advertising insert that it titled "Beachin' Times." Miller placed the insert in dozens of campus newspapers at large universities in time for spring break. Among the Miller beer ads the insert featured lush photos of scantily clad bathing beauties, violating one of the beer code's explicit taboos.

Students at the University of Wisconsin voted to censure Miller. The company then decided not to distribute any more copies of "Beachin' Times."

"SPUDS"

Another kind of youth appeal was tried by Anheuser-Busch in January 1988. The company used the dog featured in many ads for Bud Light beer, Spuds McKenzie, in ways that seemed to many to promote drinking by minors. Spuds dolls went on sale in toy stores, and children in cities and towns across the country were wearing sports shirts highlighting a drawing of Spuds and touting the good qualities of Bud Light.

Anheuser-Busch spokesmen pleaded innocent, insisting that no company products were licensed for sale to anyone under the legal drinking age. But merchandise featuring the bullterrier soon disappeared from the stores. The company no longer features the dog in its ads.

CHALLENGING THE ADS

Alcohol advertising and promotions targeting underage consumers continued to appear, and in September 1992 the Center for Science in the Public Interest filed a petition asking the Federal Trade Commission to crack down on such ads and similar marketing devices.

Fifteen national groups had signed the petition. They included the American Medical Association, the National Parent-Teachers Association, the National Council on Alcoholism, the National Council on Alcoholism and Drug Dependence, and the Southern Baptist Convention's Christian Life Commission.

The FTC had already promulgated rules against deceptive advertising and marketing. The petition called upon it to apply them to youth-oriented alcohol ads and to marketing techniques aimed at the youth market. A spokesman for the center accused the FTC of "a lack of response to marketing practices that clearly are questionable."

The complaint singles out the paid placement of alcoholic beverages in movies and in television shows. It also mentions the ads that link drinking with high-risk activities such as race-car driving. All ads of this type are supposedly forbidden by the FTC and the industry's own ethical advertising codes. Enforcement of these codes has thus far been feeble, according to the spokesman for the organizations that signed the petition.

RADIO AND TV ADS

Beer and wine ads on radio and TV cannot be aimed selectively at specific segments of the audience. All kinds of people, young and old, male and female, drinkers and teetotalers, watch most TV shows or tune in to radio programs.

This fact presents a difficult problem for liquor advertisers: How can they avoid having their ads and commercials viewed or heard by unintended audiences, particularly children? This remains an unsolvable dilemma; nor is it clear that the liquor advertisers are eager to solve it. After all, young viewers do grow up, and many become adult drinkers.

Yet there are serious issues involved here. Alcohol ads on TV and radio convincingly portray drinking as a life-enhancing activity, and one that is accepted by society as perfectly normal. Given the known vulnerability of the young to advertising, the questionable long-term effects of these ads would seem to require immediate attention by responsible authorities.

The young comprise a large part of the TV-viewing audience, and studies have shown that they watch TV in very large numbers during periods of heavy advertising. In a recent survey 68 percent of all ads for alcoholic beverages were shown during prime time (8 to 11 P.M.). A full thirty-one million youngsters between the ages of two and seventeen, or 22.7 percent of the total audience, watched prime-time TV during the period of the survey.

Nineteen million of them were two- to eleven-year-old children, and twelve million were twelve- to seventeen-year-olds.

Some 29.7 percent of alcohol commercials are customarily broadcast on Saturdays and Sundays. Most appear during sports events. According to CBS Television, football games' average viewership includes 1.9 million children and 1.7 million teenagers.

HEALTH WARNINGS

A major step was taken toward making sure that drinkers were aware of the dangers of drinking when federal law required health warnings on alcoholic beverages in late 1989.

In the summer of 1990 a subcommittee of the House of Representatives held hearings on a bill that would require health warnings to be included in all liquor advertising. They would "rotate" or change periodically, as the warnings in tobacco ads do. Ads in print media would have to carry an 800 number for counseling and referral. Broadcast ads would be read aloud by an announcer, while the text was printed out on the TV screen.

"We must ensure that people have adequate information to combat the $2 billion the [alcoholic beverage] industry spends every year to glamorize drinking," said Congressman John Conyers, Jr. (D-Michigan), a co-sponsor of the bill.

Physicians, representatives of the beer, wine, and distilled spirits industries, and spokesmen for the advertising and broadcast industries debated the bill in an all-day session. The representative of the National Association of Broadcasters argued that time-consuming health warnings would drive the industry to drop its fifteen-second TV spots. That would constitute a substantial financial loss to the TV networks.

Organizations supporting the bill include the National Parent-Teachers Association, the American Medical Association, MADD, and the Center for Science in the Public Interest.

The bill had little prospect of passing in 1990. It has been brought up again since then, but has not yet been enacted. It seems to be picking up votes, however, and was proposed in 1991 in the House by Congressman Joseph P. Kennedy II (D-Massachusetts) and in the Senate by Senator Strom Thurmond (R-South Carolina).

In 1990 Gallup did a poll for *Advertising Age* magazine. It showed that 74 percent of the public favors health warnings on TV liquor ads. Yet no version of the bill has thus far emerged from committee in either the House or the Senate.

"Alcohol advertising is the greatest single source of alcohol education for Americans," said Thurmond, "and rarely does it encourage them to consider the consequences of drinking."

Storm over Advertising to Minorities

Liquor advertisers have come under fire for their efforts to sell their products to inner-city residents, almost all African Americans and Latinos. Ads specifically designed to appeal to these groups are heavily concentrated on outdoor billboards in these neighborhoods, although they sometimes appear also in the print and broadcast media.

These intensive advertising campaigns ignore the fact that alcohol abuse is the leading health and safety problem in the African-American community. An article in the spring 1992 issue of the *Journal of Drug Issues* put it this way:

> For African-American communities, there seem to be few rules about decency, fair commercial advertising practices, and ethical behavior when it comes to advertising certain brands of alcoholic beverages. Although the advertising industry proclaims it has self-

regulation of its advertising practices, such practices are largely ignored when it comes to advertising in the African-American community.

The words and pictures used in ads are also supposedly regulated by the Bureau of Alcohol, Tobacco, and Firearms. These regulations are simply ignored by the makers of these minority community ads. Many of the ads offer indirect promises of heightened self-esteem, wealth, social acceptance, and sexual prowess. They contain no information about the risks of drinking.

When one seeks out the reasoning behind the targeting of the African-American community, it is especially interesting to note that African-American youth drink less than their white counterparts, and even less than Latino youth.

Among black youth twelve to seventeen years old, a recent survey showed that less than 20 percent used alcohol within the previous month. The rates for Hispanic and white youth were 30 and 35 percent, respectively. Of eighteen- to twenty-five-year-olds, 45 percent of the African Americans said they used alcohol in the last month. No less than 70 percent of whites of the same age, and 60 percent of Latinos, reported doing the same. A survey of all ages and both sexes showed that African Americans still drank less than whites.

To the alcohol industry, these findings mean that there is a large untapped market among blacks. They constitute a younger population than the white majority, and a faster-growing one. They are potential drinkers. The industry therefore spends millions trying to tap into this market.

But this community already suffers from a number of social, economic, and health ills. Despite the fact that

African Americans tend to drink less than whites, rates of cirrhosis of the liver, cancer of the esophagus, and other alcohol-related diseases are significantly higher for black males than for whites. African Americans also suffer from the nation's highest incidence of hypertension (high blood pressure). This ailment can easily be aggravated by alcohol.

Increased alcohol abuse is also linked to high unemployment, already a problem in the inner-city ghettos. Poor people who abuse alcohol also face a greater risk of homelessness. African Americans make up 11 percent of the population, but account for 18 percent of persons receiving alcoholism treatment.

Alcohol problems cause high rates of disease and death in African-American neighborhoods. Critics of advertising say that targeting this population with alcohol ads is economic exploitation at best, and genocide at worst.

The evidence is inconclusive, however, as to whether concentrated advertising leads to increased drinking, or whether a ban on advertising reduces drinking. But the advertising industry itself has stated that it believes African Americans are especially vulnerable to advertising claims, and they respond to ads more readily than whites.

Other researchers have found that ads may stimulate consumption by both adults and teenagers to a small but important extent. A number of studies have shown that exposure to alcohol ads does create positive attitudes toward alcohol and unrestrained drinking.

One study explored forty-two magazines, including four specially oriented to the African-American reader: *Ebony, Jet, Black Enterprise,* and *Essence.* The study sought to determine the content and distribution of magazine ads targeted at blacks. It found that almost one-eighth of the ads in the four magazines were alcohol ads, nearly double the number found in the other magazines. An alcohol ad appeared in the four magazines published for the African-American audience on the average of every fifteen pages. Readers were exposed to an abnormally high number of these ads.

Alcoholic beverage companies and the advertising industry do try to compensate for their concentrated advertising to African Americans by contributing heavily to their charitable, cultural, and athletic programs. For example: The companies provide much of the financial support for luncheons, concerts, and other celebrations honoring the memory of Dr. Martin Luther King, Jr., and Stroh's beer and Seagram donate substantial sums annually to the Martin Luther King, Jr., Center for Non-Violent Social Change in Atlanta, Georgia.

Observances like Black History Month receive extensive support from the alcohol industry. The Miller Brewing Company recently established the $1.6 million Thurgood Marshall Scholarship for young African Americans. The Anheuser-Busch Company has underwritten the Lou Rawls Parade of Stars telethon since 1979. This is the largest national fund-raiser for the United Negro College Fund.

Several companies have hired African Americans in highly visible positions as vice presidents in charge of minority affairs, public relations, and plant operations.

Though the African-American publishing community depends on the liquor industry for advertising dollars, it seeks other sources. *Essence* magazine has been outstandingly successful. Its December 1991 issue contained seventy-one pages of advertising. There were only seven alcohol ads and two cigarette ads.

In October 1991 one brewer submitted a plan to market

a new brand of malt liquor mainly to the black community. It was to be called Powermaster, a name rife with connotations supposedly attractive to minority males. But the Bureau of Alcohol, Tobacco, and Firearms disapproved the proposed name, and the brewer had to withdraw it. Inclusion of the word *power* in the name implied stronger alcohol content, a violation of federal law.

Malt liquors have an alcohol content above the 3.7 percent of the average beer. The brewers market them mainly to inner-city dwellers seeking a cheap high. Advertising campaigns for these drinks are replete with macho power claims, which allegedly appeal especially to minorities.

WHITEWASHING THE BILLBOARDS

The Detroit Planning Commission found that 55 to 58 percent of billboards in poor neighborhoods advertise liquor and tobacco products, whereas only 34 to 43 percent do so in higher-income neighborhoods.

The Reverend Calvin Butts, pastor of Harlem's Abyssinian Baptist Church, has called for a nationwide ban on liquor and tobacco billboards in minority communities. Butts subsequently led a campaign to cover alcohol- and tobacco-related billboards in Harlem with whitewash.

A black protestor calling himself simply Mandrake was the first. In January 1990 he painted over a billboard in a black neighborhood carrying a cigarette ad. Billboards were soon being whitewashed or painted over in inner cities all over the country. The activists claimed the right to take such civil disobedience actions to call attention to their cause.

Some in the African-American community disagreed with this reasoning. Benjamin Hooks, former executive director of the National Association for the Advancement of Colored People, denounced the whitewashing campaign. It conveys the message that "white people have the sense to read the signs and disregard them and black people don't." Hooks added that the whitewashing drive implied that blacks needed "special protection" against these ads.

While the antibillboard campaign was spreading, the outdoor advertising companies were split on how to deal with it. Some companies vowed to prosecute anyone who defaced their boards. Others sought to negotiate with the protesters. One company reached a compromise with the Reverend Mr. Butts. It moved tobacco and liquor ads away from schools and places of worship and replaced them with public-service ads.

In the early 1990s executives of black-owned advertising agencies told the whitewashers that their tactics would hurt African-American media companies specializing in advertising to African Americans. At about the same time, outdoor advertising companies became the targets of a barrage of criticism about the words and pictures found in ads aimed at minorities.

DO ALCOHOL ADS INCREASE DRINKING?

In 1983 the Canadian province of Saskatchewan lifted a ban on alcohol advertising that had been in effect for fifty-eight years. This gave analysts of alcohol advertising a rare opportunity to determine whether, and how much, advertising affected the consumption of alcohol. Statisticians set to work at once, measuring the changes in beer, wine, and distilled spirits sales (if any) caused by this radical change in advertising policy.

The study's main finding was that no significant change took place in either total alcohol consumption or wine consumption. Sales of beer had increased, but sales of distilled spirits decreased.

The study's conclusion was that alcohol advertising has no effect on the overall amount of alcohol sold and consumed. This conclusion left some stubborn questions unanswered: What should public policy toward alcohol advertising be? Should it be aimed at reducing or eliminating alcohol advertising as a means of preventing alcohol's known harmful effects?

The Center for Science in the Public Interest calculated that, by the time teenagers reach driving age, they have been exposed to seventy-five thousand ads for alcoholic beverages. The Federal Bureau of Alcohol, Tobacco, and Firearms surveyed teens in four states in 1986. It found a "strongly positive" relationship between exposure to advertising and the tendency to drink.

More recently, a 1990 survey of eleven- and twelve-year-olds found that 88 percent could identify Spuds McKenzie with Budweiser (Spuds was the dog formerly featured in Budweiser advertising). This was nine times as many as could identify a Coca-Cola slogan. The survey concluded that children "were more likely to have beliefs about beer consumption that are more in line with a commercial reality [e.g., fun and good times] than with a public health reality [e.g., caution and risk]."

These ads, critics say, convey subtle lessons to youth about alcohol etiquette. One comical Budweiser spot showed a drinker in a bar ordering a "light." He was handed some "light" object, such as a floor lamp. NYU media professor Neil Postman wrote about such ads: "The fully initiated drinker knows his beers and orders by brand. Knowing what he wants is an important characteristic of adulthood and masculinity."

A TIMELESS PROBLEM

The bottom line is that alcoholic beverage companies, like all businesses, need to remain profitable. The paltry millions they spend annually on public-service ads and promotional materials are dwarfed by the $2 billion they lavish annually on advertising. There is little likelihood that this imbalance will change much in the foreseeable future.

Underage drinking will doubtless remain a major battleground in the larger war over alcohol's role in society. A stronger effort in alcohol education might have some effect, but it seems unlikely to be tried in view of the current nationwide budget cuts in school health curricula and driver education programs.

Yet the ignorance of the young about alcohol is massive. A 1991 survey by the surgeon general estimated that 56 percent of junior and senior high school students did not know the legal drinking age is twenty-one. More than 2.6 million students had no idea that alcohol abuse can lead to death. Nearly a third of high school seniors in a University of Michigan survey believed there is no real danger in having four or five drinks almost every day.

On the other hand, a Gallup Youth Poll showed that 78 percent of the young believe that drinking is having a negative effect on America.

The key question is whether laws against underage drinking should be enforced strictly, or be intended merely to serve as moral principles. Campus rules about drinking have gotten tougher, but 75 percent of college officials report no improvement in alcohol-related problems. About 30 percent told the College Alcohol Survey that things had gotten worse.

"If they make the rules harder, kids will try harder to break them," said a nineteen-year-old student at Virginia Tech, in Blacksburg. "I don't think you can do anything to keep kids from drinking."

11 TARGET: YOUNG PEOPLE

(previous page)
While the number of adult
alcoholics declines, the
number of young "problem
drinkers" is on the rise, and
the age at which they start
to drink is becoming
lower and lower.
(Barbara Peacock,
FPG International)

11

PATTERNS OF BEHAVIOR

While drug use has declined somewhat among young people, alcohol has scarcely diminished in popularity. It remains youngsters' drug of choice, the nation's most persistent problem drug. A 1991 federal survey of students in eight states showed that 10.6 million of 20.7 million seventh through twelfth graders drink. Yet all states and the District of Columbia now prohibit drinking by those under twenty-one.

Federal authorities blamed underage drinking for disturbing levels of violence and emotional problems on high school and college campuses throughout the country.

Eight million of the students polled in the 1991 federal survey drink at least once a week. About 450,000 have five drinks or more at a session. When queried they commonly deny that they are alcoholics.

They rationalize, even to themselves, with phony excuses. "I'm not old enough to be an alcoholic," they say. Or, "I only drink beer." Or, "I don't get drunk every day." Or, "I'm not some bum on skid row."

Among high school seniors, 2.3 percent drink daily. The

percentage of seniors who have five or more drinks once a week has not changed since 1978. That was the year in which youngsters' drinking peaked.

To recover from patterns of alcohol abuse or alcoholism, teens need to break through these and other forms of denial. They need to reject peer pressures. They must accept the idea of treatment. Teens require the support of family and friends. In most cases their parents must be actively involved in the treatment process.

Children of alcoholic parents are four times more likely than others to become alcoholics. Youngsters returning from an in-hospital or residential treatment program often find themselves back in the same mentally and spiritually harmful environment that was a cause of their becoming alcoholics. That is one reason why so many of them sooner or later relapse into drinking.

WHEN THE YOUNG DRIVE DRUNK

In the United States, traffic accidents are the leading cause of death for people between five and thirty-four. Alcohol is involved in half of all fatal crashes. Nearly one-third of alcohol-related traffic deaths are caused by problem drinkers or alcoholics.

Drivers sixteen to twenty-four years old represent only 20 percent of all licensed drivers, but they account for 42 percent of all fatal crashes in which at least one of the drivers had been drinking.

Raising the drinking age to twenty-one has reduced per capita arrests for DUI (Driving Under the Influence) among eighteen- to twenty-year-olds by 14 percent since 1983.

States that have recently raised their excise taxes on beer

and thereby raised its price have lower death rates from motor vehicle accidents among fifteen- to twenty-four-year-olds.

Despite all these measures, drunk driving remains the most frequent crime in the United States. The death toll is still climbing. In 1987 an estimated 23,623 people died in alcohol-related crashes. Two out of five Americans will be involved in a crash of this kind at some point in their lives. One death in an alcohol-related crash takes place every twenty-two minutes.

DESIGNATED DRIVERS

Alcohol-related accidents kill eleven thousand youths aged sixteen to twenty-four each year. Half of these deaths are due to drunk driving. This age group is the only one in the United States whose life expectancy is actually declining. Accidents in which alcohol is commonly involved include drownings, suicides, violent injuries, injuries by fire, homicides, and, of course, motor vehicle accidents.

Many alcohol-related tragedies could be prevented by naming a designated driver for each group of drinkers. This idea was actually imported from Scandinavia in the mid-1980s by the Alcohol Project at Harvard University's School of Public Medicine. Fully 93 percent of Americans think it is a valuable idea, according to a 1991 Roper Poll. Gallup recently found that 78 percent would abstain from drinking and be the designated driver.

Jay Winsten, director of the Harvard program, has tested billboards in a public-service campaign keyed to the slogan The Designated Driver is the Life of the Party. The campaign tested well among young people on Martha's Vineyard.

Winsten persuaded the Writers' Guild of America to urge Hollywood writers to insert mentions of the designated driver idea into their scripts. It showed up in more than one hundred episodes of such shows as "L.A. Law," "Dallas," and "Cheers."

Though Winsten insists that the designated driver should drink *no* alcohol during an event, in actuality the designated driver is most often the least-drunk person in the group. Critics point out that the message these ads send is that "it's okay to get plastered as long as someone else is driving."

The young are particularly prone to adopt this approach. They feel they're off the hook as long as they don't have to drive. They feel they can drink without regard to any health consequences. With the perception of danger eliminated, health damage may actually be increased.

FALSE IDs

The ease with which teens can obtain fake IDs is notorious. "At least 75 percent of all college students own a fake ID, and at the bars, they hardly check them," a nineteen-year-old student at Champlain College in Burlington, Vermont, told a reporter in 1989.

A recent federal report on enforcement of drinking age laws quoted a state official: "The vendor asked for an ID. The sixteen-year-old boy—who looked sixteen—presented the ID of a five-foot four-inch female, except that he had taped his picture on it. He was a six-foot five-inch male. Nevertheless, the clerk sold him the beer."

The National Highway and Transport Safety Administration trains state officials in detecting IDs that have been fabricated, altered, or transferred to another person. Amateurish efforts to alter documents—handwriting used to replace typed data, for instance—are easier to detect, according to an NHTSA alcohol policy specialist.

Increasingly, bartenders and retail clerks are offering assistance in nullifying the use of false IDs. Courts have ruled that they are not liable for accepting an ID that looks genuine. A club in Milwaukee uses video equipment that enlarges and projects the ID image on a screen. Obvious false IDs are quickly invalidated, and the process serves as a deterrent. Other clubs offer their bouncers a bonus for confiscating false IDs.

Some forty-six states have laws against misrepresenting one's age. Holders of fake IDs in Wisconsin, for example, get their driver's licenses suspended for thirty to ninety days, plus pay a $50 fine and have to do community service.

Vermont treats the problem more lightly. A student who earned $20,000 peddling hundreds of fake IDs was fined a mere $50. The 1991 College Alcohol Survey found that only 58 percent of colleges and universities impose a fine or institutional probation on users of fake IDs.

MADD favors new and stricter laws against false IDs. A federal law, the 1982 False Identification Crime Control Act, is regarded by many as too weak. It affects only holders of at least five false documents, and applies only when the criminal crosses state lines.

THE STATES CRACK DOWN

Many states were recently debating laws designed to meet the requirements of the 1991 federal highway bill. It set up a new $20 billion grant program to reward states that enact enforcement programs for alcohol- and drug-impaired drivers.

Under this bill, states received grants if they fulfilled four out of the following five requirements:

- Revoke drunk drivers' licenses.
- Set up safety checkpoints.
- Enact laws against drunk driving.
- Establish a standard of 0.10 blood alcohol content for drunk drivers (lowered to 0.08 after three years).
- Strengthen enforcement of the legal drinking age.

To obtain grants, the states must make it illegal to carry open containers of alcohol in a moving vehicle. Repeat drunk drivers must get their license plates and car registration revoked.

About 30 states currently permit police officers to confiscate forthwith the license of a person accused of drunk driving. The National Coalition to Prevent Impaired Driving is heading a citizens' movement lobbying for administrative license revocation. Opponents of this law contend that it would violate constitutional rights to due process.

A TRAGIC SAMPLING

The March 13, 1992, edition of the *CQ Researcher* contains numerous examples of the tragedies that befell underage drinkers in a single month, December 1991. The listing was supplied by the Office of Substance Abuse Prevention, Department of Health and Human Services.

A sampling follows. The first five cases are about college drinkers, and the second five about others.

- A twenty-two-year-old Swedish tennis player, who was a student at Franklin and Marshall College, was found unconscious in his dormitory room. He died of respiratory arrest in the emergency room. His blood alcohol level was 0.40, four times the legal limit.
- A University of New Haven student was charged with vehicular manslaughter while intoxicated. His car hit a tree, killing one passenger and injuring two others.
- At the University of Idaho five students died in the fall of 1991. The emergency room at the university medical center reported that 80 percent of its cases were alcohol-related.
- Rape charges against a University of Richmond student were dropped when the victim testified that she was so drunk she didn't even know she was being sexually assaulted.
- Four University of Tennessee students were killed in a crash after a drunken birthday celebration. The driver, a twenty-year-old sophomore, was the only one wearing a seat belt, and he survived. He was charged with four counts of vehicular homicide.
- An intoxicated high school student from Orange County, North Carolina, was hit by a train. He died from a severe head injury.
- A seventeen-year-old honor student from a Trenton, New Jersey, private school drowned in a river after drinking heavily and smoking marijuana with her boyfriend.
- A sixteen-year-old Durham, North Carolina, boy was accused of homicide. While drunk, he dropped a boulder from an overpass on a woman's car, killing her.

- In New Lenox, Illinois, hosts were found liable for serving alcoholic drinks to a fifteen-year-old girl. She was drunk when she drove her car into a tree and killed a passenger.
- A sixteen-year-old boy from Wausau, Wisconsin, who got drunk on beer, was charged with arson after setting a fire that caused $400,000 in damages to a rural elementary school.

TEEN ABUSERS AND TEEN ALCOHOLICS

Teenage drinkers have rarely been drinking long enough to show the physical effects that are common in longtime problem drinkers. Few are afflicted with cirrhosis or withdrawal symptoms, such as sweating, tremors, or hallucinations.

Nevertheless, an estimated 4.6 million Americans aged fourteen to seventeen are classified as problem drinkers, according to the NIAAA. They have suffered negative consequences from drinking, such as arrest, involvement in an accident, impaired job performance, or health problems.

Alcoholism takes root early. A study by the School of Medicine at the University of Missouri-Columbia found that 80 percent of the alcoholics being studied began drinking before they were 19.1. The average age was 13, but many started as young as 9.

Minors are more likely to drink alone. This is surprising, because they are also more likely to need the approval of their peers.

Young problem drinkers resist treatment more often than adults. They are afraid of misunderstanding, restriction, punishment, rejection, or abandonment. Their denial is harder to break through because they have not experienced the consequences of heavy drinking that older people have experienced. These include divorce, job loss, or loss of child custody.

The primary focus of treatment must be the alcohol problem, but the counselors also need to provide teenage patients with basic skills they may have not yet acquired. For example, the patients will need to deal with realities like education, family, social relationships, and employment.

Alcoholic teens are approximately 20 percent of the alcoholic population in the United States. Of those fourteen to seventeen, 4.6 million are alcoholics. It makes no difference how long they have been drinking, as teens can develop the addiction very quickly.

The young who need the most help are those who started to drink the earliest. Although some children who experiment with drinking in their early teens have stopped drinking by the time they reach college, most do not. Young men and women who start drinking in college may develop drinking habits more self-destructive than those who start earlier but drink more moderately.

A recent Gallup Poll asked teenagers why they drink. Peer pressure, sometimes as early as fourth grade, was cited by 29 percent. Another 26 percent said they did it to escape from the pressures of daily living. About 15 percent drank just in order to feel good or get high. Problems at home motivated 11 percent. A group amounting to 10 percent admitted they were just showing off. Eight percent were doing it to appear grown-up.

Young drinkers were formerly thought to come from troubled homes on the wrong side of the tracks. Nowadays drinking teenagers are known to originate from families of all classes.

Among teenagers living in areas that are dependent on

cars, such as suburbs and rural areas, where there may be no movie theaters or teen centers, teenagers may drink out of sheer boredom.

For many college students as well as adults, drinking often helps to get conversation rolling. "For most students (and for nonstudents, too)," writes Lewis Eigen of the Office of Substance Abuse Prevention, "it is a lot easier to say to a friend, 'Let's go over to Benny's and hoist a few,' than it is to say, 'I'm worried about some personal problems and would like to share this with you and get some advice and sympathy.' "

Another reason for drinking is the rebelliousness that is normal in adolescence. One way or another, it usually finds expression in alcohol, drugs, or sex. It is part of the process of breaking away—from respectablilty, from conformity, from authority.

It is widely believed that alcohol is an aphrodisiac. The truth is that it has the opposite physiological effect. Alcohol does, however, tend to have the psychological effect of relaxing inhibitions. Polls of the young have shown that both males and females regard a woman who drinks as a more compliant sex partner.

Sex while under the influence is risky, especially for women. The sexual act itself may be hasty, impersonal, unemotional—and regretted later. The chances of pregnancy and/or disease are increased. An estimated 16 percent of teens who drink use condoms less often after drinking. Date rape and gang rape are more likely.

YOUNGER AND YOUNGER

According to Lloyd Johnston, a University of Michigan social science researcher who conducts a widely respected annual survey of drinking by high school and college students, "By twelve, most kids know someone who drinks." He added, "And they probably know a significant number who drink." In other words, they start to drink because they are surrounded by a drinking culture.

Dr. Johnston's survey found that 90 percent of college students have tried alcohol. Fully 75 percent drink regularly, while 4 percent drink daily. Those who had five drinks or more at one sitting within the two weeks preceding the survey came to 41 percent. In the late 1970s the figure stood at 45 percent.

The astonishing amount that college students spend on alcoholic beverages every year totals no less than $5.5 billion. A recent study found that drinking is one of the major causes of absenteeism in college. This study found that 25 percent of all student deaths are associated with alcohol. So are 90 percent of the rapes that occur on campus.

Drinking will cause more than 7 percent of 1993's freshman class—more than 120,000 students—to drop out. There are currently twelve million college students in the United States. Between 240,000 and 300,000 of them will die of alcohol-related causes.

THE PARENTS' ROLE

Parents' behavior can be decisive in determining whether a youngster will drink or not. Back in 1978 the Research Triangle Institute of North Carolina found that 59 percent of all students who had at least one parent who they believed drank regularly were heavy drinkers themselves. Teens whose parents allowed their teenage children to drink were twice as likely to drink heavily than those whose parents forbade it.

Young people who are unable to communicate well with their parents tend to engage in heavy drinking. Those with at least one parent with whom they can communicate freely are less likely to become problem drinkers.

But parents' attitudes toward their children's drinking vary widely. Some will try to organize crackdowns on drinking by youngsters. Others will criticize police when they arrest underage drinkers. They will seek to prevent their offspring's driver's license from being suspended or revoked. Often they deny that their drunken child has any kind of drinking problem.

Many parents perceive their kids' drinking as a passing stage that they went through themselves. Many are simply grateful their kids are not into illegal drugs. Some parents decline to check their children's breath, search their rooms, or impose curfews.

Several studies have sought to determine whether drinking scenes on television, in movies, and in advertising affect drinking by young people. The results have been inconclusive. But the U.S. Department of Health and Human Services, in its 1990 *Alcohol and Health Report,* warned that "the results of two studies suggest that television may influence young children's beliefs about alcohol."

Alcoholism counselors rarely advocate Prohibition as a solution. They know from firsthand experience that alcoholics must learn to quit of their own accord, and to stay sober even when alcoholic beverages are available to them.

Counselors know, too, the difficulties confronting them in the struggle to counteract the impact of glamorous and persuasive television commercials and magazine ads on the young. The counselors' jobs are rendered all the more prob-

lematic by the fact that the United States persists in classifying liquor and tobacco as legal drugs while outlawing such
substances as heroin, marijuana, and cocaine.

There is a special urgency behind the work of those who
counsel alcoholics. In the words of Dr. Nicholas A. Pace of
the National Council on Alcoholism and Drug Dependence,
"Those of us who deal with alcoholic patients every day"
realize that these individuals are "far more likely to commit
suicide or homicide or to die from strokes, certain cancers,
liver and lung disease."

THE DRUGS-ALCOHOL LINK

The industry resents any attempts to link alcohol
and drugs. The Distilled Spirits Council of the United States
(DISCUS) is especially disturbed by the "gateway theory,"
which holds that drinking often leads to abuse of hard drugs.
DISCUS dismisses as "pseudoscience" the biomedical theory that alcohol activates a pleasure center in the brain that
requires stimulants of ever-increasing power.

"The vast majority of youth who have experimented
with alcohol for decades," says DISCUS, "do so without
ever going to illegal drug use."

Anheuser-Busch, brewer of Budweiser beer, wrote a letter to shareholders pointing out some differences between
alcohol and drugs. There is no way that crack cocaine and
heroin can be used responsibly, the letter said, but alcohol
can. It also mentioned the large tax revenues that alcohol
provides to the government, in contrast to illegal drugs.

In September 1990, shortly before leaving his federal
post as drug czar, William Bennett wrote a report arguing
that a higher excise tax on alcohol would raise prices and

thus deter young people from drinking. Bennett also called alcohol a gateway drug.

This was another blow struck by the drys. Where did it leave the balance between the wets and the drys?

12 ⋮ WETS VS. DRYS: WHO IS WINNING?

1 2

....

$\mathbf{E}$arly in the nation's history, around 1820, when drinking was at its most widespread, the wets seemed triumphant. But even then, the muted voices of temperance could be heard in the land.

Drinking then entered a period of gradual decline. Through the nineteenth century the drys mustered their strength. The entry of women into the battle, especially the formation of the Woman's Christian Temperance Union in 1874, strengthened the drys enormously. After almost a century of campaigning that took many forms, the drys at long last triumphed with the enactment of Prohibition.

But the drys' victory proved short-lived. Prohibition lasted only thirteen years before it was repealed. Although a few years of increased drinking ensued, drinking eventually entered a long downward slide. At this writing the slide continues as the number of teetotalers and light drinkers rises. Fewer adults are drinking alcoholic beverages. Those who do drink are drinking more beer and less distilled spirits.

Still, there remain some deeply troubling aspects of the nation's drinking problem. Foremost among these are the patterns of behavior of the young. Their use of hard drugs has diminished in recent years, but alcohol is still their drug of choice.

Liquor advertising has developed into another problem area. It seems clear that, despite their ethical advertising codes, despite the millions they spend on public-service campaigns, the liquor companies do seek to expand the liquor market by targeting specific vulnerable elements within the population. The demand for tougher federal regulation of liquor ads is rising, but those concerned about civil liberties point out that advertising comes within the protection of the First Amendment.

It seems unrealistic to offer any firm predictions about the future course of drinking in America. This nation is too diverse for that.

The drys have won some points in terms of regulation of the liquor and liquor advertising industries by local, state, and federal governments. The American people seem hospitable to the idea of temperance, as long as it is not backed by officially imposed limitations on their freedom to drink as much, or as little, as they choose.

But Americans are quite hostile to the possible return of Prohibition in the foreseeable future. The drys are going to have to live with the fact that America is, and seemingly has every intention of continuing to be, a drinking nation. The right to drink may bring along with it many social problems, but Americans seem willing to deal with these as they arise.

As for the wets, they, too, have won some points and lost some. For example: After beating back the forces of Prohibition and regaining the freedom to drink, they have had to accept the idea of health warning labels on liquor bottles and a great variety of other kinds of liquor regulation. America may have decided to remain a drinking nation, but even wets know that the right to drink has its limits.

SUGGESTIONS
FOR FURTHER
READING

Alateen: Hope for Children of Alcoholics. New York: Alcoholics Anonymous Family Group Headquarters, 1983. A brief history of the organization, and a description of how it functions.

Alcoholics Anonymous: The Story of How Thousands of Men and Women Have Recovered from Alcoholism. 3d ed. New York: Alcoholics Anonymous World Services, Inc., 1976. A brief history of AA, with an account of its procedures. Commonly called "The Big Book."

Alibrandi, Tom. *Young Alcoholics.* New York: Comprehensive Care, 1978. Written by a former youth director, who surveys the problem and also offers good advice to parents.

Allen, Frederick Lewis. *Only Yesterday: An Informal History of the 1920s.* New York: Perennial Library Edition, 1929. A breezily written glance at the highlights and lowlifes of the period. There are more recent paperback reprints.

Black, Claudia. *It Will Never Happen to Me! Children of Alcoholics as Youngsters, Adolescents, Adults.* New York: MAC Publishing, 1982. Regarded as a classic. One of the first studies of these children and how they grow up.

———. *My Dad Loves Me, My Dad Has a Disease.* New York: MAC Publishing, 1982. The children of alcoholics, ages six to fourteen, express their feelings in words and pictures.

Christopher, James. *How to Stay Sober: Recovery Without Religion.* New York: Prometheus, 1988. Argues that it is possible to recover from alcoholism without a belief in a Higher Power.

Claypool, Jane. *Alcohol and Teens.* New York: Messner, 1985. A brief discussion, written for young readers.

Fleming, Alice. *Alcohol, the Delightful Poison: A History.* New York: Delacorte, 1975. Amusingly written and informative, but only partly about the U.S.

Hornik-Beer, Edith L. *A Teen-Ager's Guide to Living with an Alcoholic Parent.* Minneapolis: Hazelden, 1984. Answers questions about how to cope.

Hyde, Margaret. *Alcohol: Uses and Abuses.* Hillside, N.J.: Enslow, 1988. A useful survey, written for young readers.

Jacobson, Michael. *The Booze Merchants: The Inebriating of America.* Washington, D.C.: Center for Science in the Public Interest, 1983. Well-written, illustrated study of liquor advertising.

Lang, Alan R. *Alcohol: Teenage Drinking.* New York: Chelsea House, 1985. A brief analysis, written for young people.

Lender, M. E., and J. K. Martin. *Drinking in America: A History.* New York: Free Press, 1982. One of the first complete histories of the subject.

Lerner, Katherine. *Something's Wrong in My House.* New York: Franklin Watts, 1988. Children of different ethnic and cultural backgrounds tell how it feels to be children of alcoholics.

Living Sober: Some Methods AA Members Have Used for Not Drinking. New York: Alcoholics Anonymous World Services, Inc., 1975. A guidebook with thirty tips on how to stay sober.

Rorabaugh, W. J. *The Alcoholic Republic: An American Tradition.* Oxford: Oxford University Press, 1970. A lively history of drinking in the U.S. up to about 1840.

Shuker, Nancy. *Everything You Need to Know about an Alcoholic Parent.* New York: Rosen Group, 1989. Helpful advice for young people.

"Underage Drinking." *CQ Researcher,* March 13, 1992.

Wholey, Dennis. *The Courage to Change.* Boston: Houghton Mifflin, 1984. Celebrities tell their own stories of alcoholism and recovery.

Yoder, Barbara. *The Recovery Resource Book.* New York, Fireside, 1990. An immensely helpful guide to resources on all forms of addiction and co-dependency.

INDEX

Page numbers in *italics* indicate illustrations.